AMERICAN POLICY FOR PEACE
IN THE MIDDLE EAST

AMERICAN POLICY FOR PEACE IN THE MIDDLE EAST 1969-1971

Problems of Principle, Maneuver and Time

Robert J. Pranger

American Enterprise Institute for Public Policy Research
Washington, D. C.

Robert J. Pranger is a resident scholar of the American Enterprise Institute for Public Policy Research.

Foreign Affairs Study 1, December 1971

Library of Congress Catalog Card No. L.C. 70-188039

Printed in United States of America

CONTENTS

INTRODUCTION

Between Tel Aviv and the Jordan River lies a chain of hills covered with stones and stone fences. It is a sight that has inspired some to say that when God created the earth, He filled Palestine with stones and thus bequeathed to successive generations living there a legacy of interminable labor. Northward in Lebanon, at the site of ancient Byblos, stands a remarkable archeological record of faded cultures dating back to the origins of time, a perspective on history that fills the spectator with a humble sense of how ancient the Middle East is. Yet in Cairo and Riyadh, as in other major Middle Eastern cities, modernity presses forward in the fantasies of urban demolition and construction. Meanwhile, in Israeli *kibbutzim* near the Jordan River and in Arab villages and towns on the river's east bank, residents still fear the advent of new warfare. Such are the stubborn, enduring realities of the Middle East: its tenacious peoples, its ancient memories, its modern aspirations, and its spasmodic wars.

Against the background of these inescapable realities, however, there persists a contemporary political drama that is more fluid, more open for improvisation, than some might think. If destiny consists, in part, of historical necessity, it still opens future opportunities as well. It is public policy's greatest challenge to enlarge upon such choices as seem possible in given circumstances, rather than to drown in the drift of diffident realities. Indeed, what distinguishes politics from the more strictly managerial arts are the active and latent opportunities it offers for charting new courses in public action. That politicians in the Middle East seem always to play before the same audiences, recite approximately the same lines, and use the same scenery does not mean that politics in the Middle East is frozen into meaningless rituals where puppets move by superhuman design. In

1

fact, the fondness displayed by Middle Easterners for metaphors of inevitable fate has consistently masked a fluidity in the region's politics that often catches observers unprepared to take advantage of situations as they develop.

More than in Europe or the United States, however, audiences, rituals and scenes in the Middle East do have extraordinary influence on the political activity of insiders and outsiders. There exists a powerful inertial pull from entrenched habits of mind that must be counteracted by equally strenuous efforts, if new paths for political development are to remain open. Despite the ageless hyperactivity of various outside powers in the Middle East, its peoples remain persistently endogenous. Western culture has visible impact everywhere, yet historical memories specific to the region linger among Arabs and engender enthusiasm among Israelis. Even modern war's tendency to forge a total unity between frontline and homefront is hampered in the Middle East by the cake of custom, especially the strong centrifugal forces of poverty and privacy. These forces make a war of attrition unattractive, a surprise kill exciting. The dangers for the area and the world from such locally preferred strategies of warfare allying themselves with the patronage of the two superpowers who can pursue total war strategies need little elaboration. The description of this alliance as a powderkeg furnishes one of those rare analogies that fits perfectly.

In no sector of political action is the pull of the environment more apparent than in the international relations of the Middle East, and nowhere in these relations is the struggle between inertia and innovation more dramatic than in the conflict between Israel and the Arabs. Surely the visibility of this struggle is a powerful, if latent, impulse toward an ultimate settlement of the conflict; but this same, almost catatonic stalemate between lassitude and change is symptomatic of how difficult such a settlement will be to achieve.

Wartime legacy and economic necessity have compelled the United States to involve itself deeply in both the inertia and innovation of the Middle East—in its cultures, economies and politics. Since early 1969, President Nixon and his chief advisers have wrestled with various formulae for a peace settlement between Israel and the Arabs on the grounds that this conflict cannot help but affect negatively American prospects in the region and perhaps globally. In the process of this search for solutions, some promising avenues to peace have been discovered. At the same time, however, these U.S. efforts have occasionally contributed to the strength of the inertial factors that threaten to bring Israel and the Arabs to full warfare once again.

A central theme of this study will be that the most significant steps toward peace in the Middle East during the past three years have occurred when innovation has made inertia serve its purposes. Here the true genius of a "balanced" American policy becomes apparent: the thrust of balance is not to reconcile contradictory policies toward Israel and the Arabs under the rubrics of national interest and global strategy, but to make local contradictions work in harness for the larger objectives of U.S. national security, international stability and eventual peace. In this sense, the Middle East represents a microcosm, a "case study," that proves instructive for national security policy in general: American policy has contributed handsomely to peace in the Middle East during the past three years when it has been based on a patiently contrived synthesis between fundamental purpose and opportunistic maneuver, a synthesis reinforced by the adroit use of time.[1] Here, the national interests of peace and security have been served by a policy without homogeneous structure. On the other hand, where American policy has unsuccessfully coped with, or even encouraged, lethargy in the Middle East, it has neglected the fine balances between purpose, maneuver and time, turning instead to an overemphasis on parts of the balance. This does not suggest, of course, that this synthesis was consciously pursued on all occasions or even most successful when most conscious. On the other hand, this was not a muddled policy of drift.

By late 1971, however, the normal patterns of Middle East politics have asserted themselves: shadowy stories of new arms deals with Moscow and Washington, impassioned rhetoric in the United Nations, fateful prognoses about inevitable war, and learned discussions on the Middle East arms "balance" by strategists who ignore the possibility that both sides dream of and plan for decisive advantage, not stalemate. Setbacks immediately after the cease-fire's initiation in August 1970 were predictable, but there also existed signs that the truce would start a new, more constructive, chain of events in directions as then unclear. Despite subsequent proposals for an interim settlement, however, no significant progress toward peace has been made since the cease-fire took effect, and now Arabs and Israelis are predicting the worst. The synthesis appears on the verge of falling apart. For this reason, it seems a good time to make more explicit the policy of balanced relations and to recommend some possibilities for renewed negotiations.

---

[1] This is not to ignore that the Middle East is atypical for American policy in at least one respect, the strong domestic support for Israel.

This study will deal with the following three topics. First, the major decisions in American Middle East policy in the period from early 1969 to late 1971 will be reviewed, with some judgment as to how and why these decisions contributed to innovation or encouraged inertia. Key events within the Middle East in this same period, including graduated Soviet efforts on Egypt's behalf, will be examined in the light of these decisions. Obviously, decisions and events are closely related, but they are never in complete congruence. Second, the present field of forces in the Middle East, partly an outgrowth of decisions and events during the previous three years, will be described and prospects for peace assessed. Finally, in the light of the latter assessment, recommendations for further American policy initiatives will be proposed.

One final comment about the purpose and approach of this study. This is not an analysis of so-called "realities" in the Middle East, of which the author is quite aware, but of peacemaking efforts by the United States in the region. Or better put, this essay addresses the issue of how a policy of peace can be developed in the midst of contrary realities. It will come as no surprise that such a policy is almost, but not quite, utopian. It is for the sake of this "not quite" that this study is written. Familiar arguments will be marshalled against what is proposed here. So as not to anticipate these objections, however, they will simply be ignored in the less-than-realistic hope that an innovative American option directed toward lasting peace in the ' Middle East still remains a possibility. But the reader should make no mistake: the author understands the realities only too well, and he also deplores them from the standpoint of the interests of both the United States and the Middle East. From any perspective—economic, military or political—there is nothing beneficial in a war that leads only to great tragedy, as this one would be bound to do.

The author will not, therefore, grace the familiar arguments against peace in the Middle East with such descriptions as "realistic" or "sophisticated." It is better to ignore them, knowing however, that these tired formulae of inevitable conflict between Arabs and Israelis will naturally reassert themselves. Thus, this study will try to approach American policy toward the Middle East in terms of implementing a paramount *American* interest in peace. More typically, American interests in the area have been analyzed in terms of confrontation with the U.S.S.R, or saving Israel, or preserving access to Arab oil, or staying out of another inevitable war between Israel and the Arabs.

The approach set forth here adds a fifth option, one that has been quite consciously pursued on occasion over the past three years —that of making peace to the material and spiritual benefit of the United States. In this sense, the United States needs peace not simply to protect worldwide investments or to shield client states or to thwart the Soviet Union, but to convince itself that its international commitments over the past years have not been in vain: that the good of mankind has been served by extensive United States activities in the world and that its own domestic society has benefited. The United States badly needs a sense of national pride in the handiwork of its international policies, a feeling that these policies do indeed work for the positive aims of advancing American and international welfare. Success for United States peace efforts in the Middle East would provide at least one step toward such pride.

1

DECISIONS, 1969

Because they will be finally tested in the complicated arena of international maneuver, all national security decisions have a certain tentativeness. But even dramatic refutation of a decision by subsequent events must still be reassimilated by those who will sit in final judgment on what changes, if any, should be made in the policy. In Susanne K. Langer's words "the brain is not merely a great transmitter, a superswitchboard; it is better likened to a great transformer."[1] The mind first creates decisions, and then acts as a screen through which any experience that might contradict such decisions must pass.

Hence it seems proper to begin a study on Middle East policy with the *reasons* decisions have been made, as will be done here, which is a rather separate question from what overall factors compel decisions to be made. The Middle East's fascination with metaphors of destiny, magnified by the U.S.S.R. with its own strong allegiance to historical inevitability, tends to divert attention toward compulsion and away from purposive action. Once attention is so diverted, self-fulfilling prophecies go to work. If one falls into this ideological trap, then a balanced policy that blends principle, maneuver and time proves impossible to achieve; one becomes prisoner of the policies and prophecies of others.

When decisions have been implemented "out there" in the arenas of political activity, they take on the conventional cloak of public policy and come into contact with the policies of others. The latter policies also emerge from whatever reasoning lies behind decisions, a reasoning that is, to some extent, independent of the reasons that

---

[1] *Philosophy in a New Key* (New York: Mentor Books, 1958), p. 46.

guide other actors. Once policy can be seen operating in real time, corrections may be made, if circumstance and judgment permit. In sum, there exists a complicated and fluid field of tangled reasons, decisions, policies, results and assessments. This jumbled field makes it extremely difficult, if not impossible, to judge what is "realistic," "successful" and "right" policy at any given time. It also prohibits the use of "mirror images" in order to gauge the intentions of others. Asymmetry among policies and disjunction between events become commonplace, while traditional linear images of cause and effect, as well as stimulus and response, lose much of their relevance.[2]

Sometimes there are decisions that come to represent fundamental shifts in national security policy both for those making the decisions *and* for those to whom the decisions are addressed (which may be more a matter of dramatic impact than real substance). At this point, possibilities open for "initiatives" in the policy field. But it is characteristic of such initiatives that they easily become ephemeral gestures unless "followed up" by planned steps that add to the weight of their impact. A "major breakthrough" in foreign affairs would result from opportunities being converted into initiatives and initiatives into genuine realignments of factors previously considered more or less permanently arranged in another pattern (insofar as anything in politics can be permanent). Rather than speaking of national security policy as dominating the field or keeping a status quo intact, it would perhaps be more appropriate to see such policy as largely an exploratory enterprise, with no special powers of transcendence—a policy that seeks to make enough impact on the field to influence within varying degrees of comprehensiveness the activities of other actors. Factors of judgment *within the midst* of events would become more important than factors of control *over* events. Such an approach to policy is, however, far removed from the more masterful images of American security policy proposed over the past 20 years.[3]

As will be noted in the review of major decisions from early 1969 to late 1971, some significant initiatives were made by the United States in this period. However, they were not followed by further steps so that one could speak meaningfully of a major breakthrough toward peace in the Middle East. The one possible exception to this

---

[2] See the basic discussion of the "phenomenal field" (*le champ phénoménal*) in Maurice Merleau-Ponty, *Phénoménologie de la perception* (Paris: Gallimard, 1945), pp. 64-77; and of the "political field" in Robert J. Pranger, *Action, Symbolism, and Order* (Nashville: Vanderbilt University Press, 1968), pp. 35-53.

[3] The contrasts will be explored more fully in the author's forthcoming book, *The Structure of National Defense Policy.*

generalization was the movement from an *accomplished* cease-fire to a *proposed* interim settlement based on opening the Suez Canal. Surely the cease-fire has proved to be an initiative latent with further possibilities for settlement of the Arab-Israeli conflict, and, because of this, the most important American initiative of the past three years. To show what possibilities might be explored further, in order to capitalize on the cease-fire as an initiative toward peace rather than merely a breathing spell between wars, is the purpose of the recommendations made at the end of this study.

The idea of a policy field—with its tangled decisions, its fluid mixture of purpose, maneuver and time, and its potential for initiative, follow-up and breakthrough as well as for inertia—provides a useful context for discussing the most significant American decisions made on Middle East policy between early 1969 and late 1971. These decisions were by no means always congruent with events taking place in the Middle East during this same period; occasionally, American decisions were responsive, but at times they were made independently in terms of longer range factors or for the conscious purpose of introjecting new initiatives into the field of forces. Perhaps there were also events that called for "decisive action" in which the United States failed to make any decision whatsoever. Decisions were made in accordance with the inner dynamics of an *American* policy, dynamics that did emphasize maneuver and timing in terms of other actors, but dynamics that were also dictated by purposes unique to the United States. Each of the decisions reviewed below exhibited, however, its own special emphasis.

Eight critical decisions, arranged chronologically, are examined here for their impact on the field of forces in the Middle East: (1) the decision in early 1969 to negotiate bilaterally with the U.S.S.R. for a peace settlement; (2) the Rogers Plan for settlement in December 1969; (3) the decision in March 1970 to delay a final answer to Israel's latest request for more F-4s; (4) the cease-fire in August 1970; (5) the Egyptian violations of the cease-fire and American responses to these violations; (6) the abortive Jarring mission and the American decision to become an active intermediary; (7) the Jordanian crisis and United States involvement; and (8) the interim settlement plans pertaining to the Suez Canal and further steps toward peace and withdrawal.

Negotiations With the U.S.S.R. During 1969

An especially seductive myth has persisted for some time that, where the United States and the U.S.S.R. share a common rivalry, they also

9

have a mutual interest in negotiating an end to or stabilizing that rivalry. Yet of all the *reasons* to negotiate, rivalry may be the least compelling, as long as either side sees an advantage in continuing the competition. This is all the more true when one party thinks that such rivalry is inevitable or when the competition is, in turn, exacerbated by conflicts between other powers. However dangerous the Soviet Union may consider its rivalry with the United States in the Middle East, particularly in its drive for Arab allegiances, it has never demonstrated much willingness to end or stabilize it—although it has evidenced some reluctance to see the rivalry get out of control.

It was a combination of assessments that led the United States into presenting negotiable proposals for full settlement of the Arab-Israeli conflict to Moscow in 1969. Aside from the fact that Russian approaches spanned the last days of the previous administration, one of the paramount principles underlying these overtures was a judgment that the Soviet Union was interested in stabilizing its rivalry with the United States in the Middle East. Since the United States wished to avoid direct confrontation with the Soviet Union, there was thought to exist a unity or symmetry of somewhat negative purposes between Moscow's and Washington's objectives in the region.

This central assessment of Soviet interest, which was deemed to be in congruence with the peaceful intentions of the United States, lay at the base of efforts to seek a joint settlement package that someone would eventually present to Israel and the Arabs for their final negotiations. While the American plan was flexible and necessarily tentative, Israel and the Arabs remained suspicious that their patrons envisaged a diplomatic *fait accompli.* Naturally, the patrons assured their respective clients to the contrary. In the Arab case, however, the U.S.S.R. nurtured suspicion of American proposals with public statements that these proposals were pro-Israeli, and thus designed to gain U.S.-Soviet accord "on everything acceptable to Israel in the shape of complete formulations while the unacceptable points should be simply turned over for direct Arab-Israeli negotiations, which are planned to take place while Israel still occupies Arab lands." For the sake of a "just peace," however, the Soviet Union could not accept any such plans as these.[4]

Even as the Department of State's painstakingly conceived proposals were presented to stoical Soviet officials in Washington and Moscow, Israel and the Arabs began escalating both the physical and

---

[4] Maksimov article in *Pravda*, January 27, 1970, quoted in *New York Times* (January 28, 1970).

psychological dimensions of their real war. In July 1969, President Nasser, apparently acting with Russian encouragement and most certainly without Russian discouragement, declared that Egypt was now embarked on the "liberation stage" of its war of attrition with Israel. Operating with a view to besting Nasser at his own game and with a curious insouciance about Soviet reactions, Israel quickly molded its newly acquired Phantom jets into a powerful combat arm to reach deep into Egyptian territory. The United States worked strenuously to promote its settlement package among the Russians, British, French, Arabs and Israelis, and focused all its major efforts on this approach until December 1969, when Secretary of State Rogers made his dramatic statement on peace in the Middle East, the so-called "Rogers Plan."

Its approach to peace through broad proposals placed the United States in a highly principled but abstract position regarding the activities of the Arab states, Israel and the U.S.S.R. As will be noted below, the same generalization can be applied to the Rogers Plan. Both sets of proposals—in negotiations with the Soviet Union and uni-laterally—proved to be many steps ahead of the game in 1969: in football terminology, short yardage was needed, not the long pass. While Washington drafted possible terms for a final settlement, hostilities intensified dangerously. As United States negotiators talked peace, Israel and Egypt, as well as Israel and Jordan, exchanged battle casualties. Indeed, at each turn in these negotiations, as amended American plans were put forward, Moscow countered with its adamant demand for full Israeli withdrawal from territories occupied in 1967 before peace negotiations could begin in earnest. Unlike Washington, Moscow carried its own version of the negotiations directly to the Arabs at every opportunity, an effort culminating in a vigorous policy statement carried in *Pravda* on January 27, 1970.

If anything, the Soviet plan presented in *Pravda* provided an even tighter "package settlement" than the American proposals did. More indicative of Russian interests in settlement at this time, however, was *Pravda's* unveiling of certain tentative American proposals made confidentially during 1969; these were cast in such a light within the context of the larger Soviet package as to serve Russian interests among the Arabs.[5] Although the article was comparatively moderate in tone, arguing that a political settlement was both desirable and

---

[5] The *Pravda* article followed by almost two months Secretary Rogers' settlement plan of December 9, 1969, a proposal greeted with some enthusiasm in the Arab world but with severe criticism in Israel.

possible, it did point out that United States proposals sought "to provide grounds for certain changes in the map of the Middle East" that were "absolutely unacceptable." The U.S.S.R., it said, favored no changes at all from the pre-June 1967 frontiers. It reiterated the Soviet position that the United States plan was firm only on everything acceptable to Israel, while leaving matters unacceptable for direct negotiation between Israel and the Arabs. Moscow demanded full Israeli withdrawal "to preclude the possibility of territorial concessions to the aggressor." [6]

Ultimately, the idea of a negotiated package settlement with the U.S.S.R. was abandoned because escalating warfare in the Middle East ruled out such an elaborate plan. Also important was the fact that the United States, by proceeding from its own interpretation of Security Council Resolution 242 of 1967 (which called for Israeli withdrawal and a peace settlement), immediately barred an agreement with the U.S.S.R. because the latter did not interpret the resolution as the Americans did. On the other hand, to have ignored the resolution entirely would only have invited Soviet reference to it. Leaving aside conflicting interpretations of United Nations resolutions (Resolution 242 was born of compromise and bound to be contentious), all actors except the United States apparently preferred to drift with lassitude in the hope of gaining some marginal or even major advantage from protracted war.

During the kind of escalation of hostilities that occurred in 1969 and late into 1970, there should have been cautious supply of military equipment by the Americans and Russians instead of the steady flow of armaments that actually took place. But again, the U.S.S.R. saw advantages in this rivalry between arms suppliers that outweighed simple prudence. American reasons for peace and Soviet reasons for competition did not coincide but were perhaps even in conflict, especially if both policies aimed, at least in part, for Arab goodwill.

As they fought over the withdrawal issue, Israel and the Arabs quite naturally increased rather than decreased their requests for more American and Soviet arms. In the fall of 1969 Israeli military representatives, with Prime Minister Meir at their head, arrived in

---

[6] *New York Times* (January 28, 1970). This was but a small token of bitter Soviet accusations, with equally startling Israeli rejoinders, that have escalated in their intensity. For example, see the angry, personal clash between the Soviet and Israeli ambassadors to the United Nations on September 26, 1971, as reported in the *New York Times* (September 27, 1971).

Washington with a long shopping list topped by F-4 and A-4 aircraft. High-ranking Egyptians frequented Moscow for additional arms.

Experience with the packaged proposal approach during 1969 taught the United States a valuable lesson for the following year: the complicated Middle East field could not be packaged in any way mutually acceptable to the United States and the U.S.S.R., however useful this approach was for keeping the two superpowers in constant contact at the level of amicable negotiations. It might be possible to deal superficially with geographical issues this way. But the Middle East's boundaries of "political space," in terms of reasons, decisions, policies, results and assessments, could not be easily contained by tidy proposals. Between Arabs and Israelis, geographical questions have always been subordinated to matters of a more profound political space, where an obvious, manifest perception of national interest merges with latent, subconscious anxieties. More central to the long stalemate between the Arabs and Israel have been these deeper issues, a field of historic, contradictory positions with many hedges against change. As 1970 began, the time for America's search for peace to explore this dangerously ambiguous terrain was at hand. In the end, the great discovery was the cease-fire of August 1970, a simple initiative, but one that promised to harness inertial forces by using, rather than ignoring, such forces. Reverting to football once again, short yardage may lead to a sustained drive. Between late 1969 and late 1970, however, lay some dangerous frustrations.

The Rogers Plan

At some point during the exchanges with the U.S.S.R. in 1969 the United States decided to surface its peace formula publicly. Whatever the reasons for this decision—they were complicated ones aimed, in part, at making a significant enough imprint on inertial forces in the Middle East policy field to unsettle everyone's plans—a speech by Secretary of State William P. Rogers on December 9, 1969 provided the occasion for public disclosure of an American plan handed to Soviet Ambassador Dobrynin on October 28.[7] The major proposals contained in the secretary's address have subsequently become identified with his policy toward the Middle East, the so-called "Rogers Plan." In terms of sheer dramatic impact on the Middle East policy

---

[7] Address to the Galaxy Conference on Adult Education, Washington, D. C. A good commentary on this address was an early one by the Washington columnists, Rowland Evans and Robert Novak, *Washington Post* (December 19, 1969).

field, the December 9 speech became the most significant United States move from early 1969 until the cease-fire appeal in mid-1970. Because it was a unilateral statement, however, the plan's weight was indeterminable as an "initiative" that might lead to subsequent agreements among parties to the conflict. And its comprehensiveness, reflecting the wide sweep of the settlement proposals given to the Soviet leadership, was not easy to translate into discreet "phases" by which small steps toward peace might open wider avenues. For this reason, the cease-fire of 1970 offered a step *toward* peace, while the Rogers Plan presented a whole policy *about* peace.[8]

Nevertheless, the December 9 proposals remain the single most important public statement on Middle East policy by President Nixon's administration, a general policy that has been affected by subsequent decisions and events, but not superseded by them. Some have argued that events in 1970 and 1971 have led to the "demise" of the Rogers policy.[9] However, this is not the secretary's perception: in his address to the U.N. General Assembly of October 4, 1971, he still held close to the central features of his plan, while adding the new elements of cease-fire and interim settlement. In other words, his public emphasis remains on full implementation of Security Council Resolution 242 of 1967 (which he describes as a major step toward peace) under United Nations auspices and the good offices of Ambassador Jarring.[10]

In brief, Secretary Rogers provided, in his December 9 address, an outline for what he termed a "balanced" policy: "to encourage the Arabs to accept permanent peace based on a binding agreement and to urge the Israelis to withdraw from occupied territory when their territorial integrity is assured as envisaged by the Security Council resolution." [11] Addressing the issues of peace and withdrawal, Mr. Rogers described the United States position on Security Council Resolution 242 as one of peace between the disputants, security for all, and

---

8 There is no reference in the secretary's December 9 address to an initiative; it is a set of proposals. In fact, in his October 4, 1971 address to the United Nations he sees Security Council Resolution 242 and the 1970 cease-fire as the two major steps toward peace in the Middle East, and proposes the opening of the Suez Canal as the third. See *New York Times* (October 5, 1971).

9 For example, *Orbis* XV (Summer 1971), p. 483.

10 This point was not ignored by Prime Minister Meir in her biting Knesset attack of October 26 on the secretary's speech to the U.N. See *New York Times* (October 27, 1971).

11 Department of State pamphlet, "A Lasting Peace in the Middle East: An American View" (1969), p. 4.

only "insubstantial alterations" in the 1949 boundaries of Israel. On the last point, the United States does not support "expansionism." [12]

In addition to the issues of peace and withdrawal, the secretary also noted that the United States did not accept "unilateral actions by any party" to decide the final status of Jerusalem, nor would it condone any settlement that did not take into account "the desires and aspirations of the refugees and the legitimate concerns of the governments in the area." [13]

Concluding his address, Mr. Rogers referred to the "new formulas" the United States had been exploring with the U.S.S.R. "in an attempt to find common positions." Each formula, he indicated, consisted of three elements: (a) a binding commitment by Israel and the U.A.R. to peace with each other; (b) a mediating effort by Ambassador Jarring, utilizing procedures similar to those used by Dr. Bunche at Rhodes in 1949 during his mediation efforts between Israel and the Arabs, to work out "detailed provisions of peace relating to security safeguards" (primarily Sharm al-Shaykh, demilitarized zones in accordance with Resolution 242, and final arrangements for the Gaza Strip); and (c) "in the context of peace and agreement of specific safeguards, withdrawal of Israeli forces from Egyptian territory...." [14]

By a quirk of fate, Secretary Rogers addressed the Galaxy Conference exactly one year to the day after Governor William Scranton, who had just finished a fact-finding trip to the Middle East for President-elect Nixon, made his controversial promise that the new administration's policy for the Middle East would be an "even-handed" one. The storm following Mr. Rogers' proposals made the Scranton embroglio minor by comparison.

As already observed, a "balanced" policy can mean something other than the even-handed approach exemplified in the secretary of state's December 9 speech. While the address was heavy on the purposes of United States policy in the Middle East—even painfully candid about matters of principle—it provided no incentives for further maneuvering. It did not mention what steps, such as a cease-fire, might prove necessary to implement the plan. Apparently, further exploration would be undertaken.

Israel reacted angrily to the secretary's address: it wished to hold the occupied territories as bargaining chips for a game of national security interests between the Arabs and Israelis in which there would

---

[12] Ibid., p. 6.

[13] Ibid., p. 7.

[14] Ibid., p. 9.

be no preconditions. Hence any comprehensive settlement package was—and still is—automatically unacceptable to Israel. A possible scenario for settlement gambits might be appropriate, but a set of comprehensive terms never. This position has remained absolutely firm as late as Mrs. Meir's October 26 attack on Secretary Rogers' address of October 4, 1971 to the United Nations.[15] This idea of a peace settlement as a grim game of negotiators with high stakes and no predetermined outcome must be reckoned with in any American peace proposal designed to win voluntary Israeli acquiescence. As events moved along in 1970 and 1971, it became obvious that American policy would have more difficulty with this demand than with almost any other policy at work in the Middle East.[16]

Privately, many Arabs applauded the Rogers Plan as a move by the United States "in the right direction," but seemed more than a little curious about how it was to be activated so as to gain Israeli support. Surely the strong Israeli statements against the plan did not augur well for its fulfillment. Further, Arab curiosity was all the more piqued by the question of how the United States would respond to Israel's request for additional Phantom jets—and particularly whether American pressure would be exerted, in any new Phantom deal, to gain Israeli acceptance of the Rogers Plan. Having sensed a shift in U.S. policy, the Arabs now asked "for deeds as well as words." In reality, most Arabs doubted that Israel with its superior military position in the Middle East, would ever accept peace terms that had been proposed by outsiders and which Israel considered "treasonous" to Israeli interests. Further, in the Middle East's tangled field of self-fulfilling prophecies, Israel's obduracy could not help but be reinforced by *Al-Goumhouria's* December 11 observation that the U.A.R. had already rejected on November 6 the terms of the Rogers proposals. How to give private applause for what one has already publicly debunked is one of those never-ending contradictions in Middle East politics; and every such contradiction fertilizes another hedgerow against the impetus of change.

In sum, the Rogers Plan was balanced in its perspectives, but unbalanced in terms of how it mixed purpose, maneuver and timing. Principles were well-articulated and still remain the bedrock of American goals in the Middle East conflict between Israel and the Arabs;

---

[15] *New York Times* (October 27, 1971).

[16] This is not to ignore that some Israelis are completely uninterested in withdrawing from the occupied territories, seeing instead the need for physical security buffers being paramount in a situation where they think real peace with the Arabs is impossible.

yet no impetus to maneuver, in order to meet the plan's objectives, was possible as long as the formulae for implementation were so vague and the sequence of events depended upon Ambassador Jarring's efforts. The first hint that the United States might be thinking in terms of its own maneuver in the political space of the Middle East, in an attempt to gain short yardage with the aim of launching a sustained drive, came on March 23, 1970: Secretary Rogers announced an American delay in a final decision on Israel's request for more Phantom jets—explained as an "interim decision" not to grant the request—in the hope that restraint might enhance the prospects of peace.

Meanwhile, during late 1969 fighting raged between Israel and the Arabs on two fronts. On November 4, an Israeli Mirage jet made a low-level pass over Cairo, a symbolic prelude to Israel's F-4 Phantom strikes deep into Egypt during 1970. Perhaps more ominous for the future, and especially for expanded Soviet military presence in Egypt, was the public declaration by a high-ranking Israeli military officer on November 10 that all Egyptian ground-to-air missile sites along the Suez Canal had been destroyed by Israel's intensive bombing raids since September. If true, this would no doubt compel the Egyptians to seek further Soviet assistance for their air defense.

As if to dramatize the growing Soviet coolness toward any comprehensive settlement, the U.S. Department of State announced on December 23, only two weeks after Secretary Rogers had made public the American proposals of October 28 to the U.S.S.R., that the Soviet reply was not "constructively responsive." For the time being, the U.S.S.R. found the rivalry between inertial forces, groaning under a tragic war, more compelling for maneuver than a peace settlement that would have to defy these forces. After a year of negotiating with the United States, the U.S.S.R. decided, either in late 1969 or early 1970 (a matter of considerable dispute), that Egypt's pressing military deficiencies required a greater Soviet involvement. This represented a decision for the status quo that was, in the Middle East context, a decision for further instability. Regardless of just when the U.S.S.R. decided to make new military commitments to Egypt, it seems probable that the Soviet move to develop and help operate a peerless air defense system was made on the basis of Egyptian military deficiencies and Israeli strengths, and *not* because the United States was pursuing its independent, potentially innovative, path to peace.

Since peace in the Middle East was of paramount American interest, yet represented a change from entrenched patterns of conflict, American policymakers wisely recognized they would have to undertake a line of action considerably separate from the activities of the U.S.S.R. Here the United States was forced to eschew the temptation, always seductive for American policy since 1945, of countering the U.S.S.R. with a comparably "tough" posture because of concern that if the Soviet Union were not backed down by force, it might move to take over the Middle East through "salami slicing" tactics. A more independent course of action required creativity and patience in the face of heavy odds made quite formidable in 1970 by the greatly expanded Soviet military activity in Egypt.[17] Without such a policy, however, there would never have developed the cease-fire of 1970 and there might well have occurred even more serious difficulties during 1970 and 1971 than actually did take place. To have done less, to have succumbed to the magic of Cold War confrontation, would have meant the end of a creative, independent and vigorous American policy in the Middle East, a diminution of American national security interests rather than an expansion of them.[18]

---

[17] Not only did the odds against Arab acceptance mount, but Israel's position also hardened with expanding Soviet presence at its doorstep.

[18] It is a measure of how strong these myths remain that the entire lexicon of Communist threat is now being applied, by some, to the Middle East. Instead of seeing the opportunities for a strong security policy in the asymmetry of relationships in the Middle East, some now have subsumed everything under a global struggle between the U.S. and U.S.S.R. for strategic balance, with the Eastern Mediterranean and the Indian Ocean the keys to this struggle. There are no limits, of course, to applying this point of view and seeing just what one wants to see. But it is a poor guide for strong, independent action in international security affairs.

2
DECISIONS, 1970

Immediately following Taiwan's expulsion from the United Nations, James Reston analyzed the hostile United States reaction to this turn of events in the context of President Nixon's seemingly contradictory efforts to improve relations with Peking.[1] Reston criticized the "deplorable and self-defeating" American tactics in the U.N. on Taiwan's behalf for having cost President Nixon "influence in the world" even as he "picked up popularity at home." Observing the contemporary mood of American frustration over world affairs, he urged that the United States be careful not "to pull away too far and in the process threaten the delicate balance of power in the world." According to Reston, "even the most casual analysis of Communist objectives" will show that, more than anything else, Communist countries seek "the reduction of U.S. involvement in the world, and if possible the return of American isolationism." The United States "is no longer in a position to pressure other nations ... into doing what they think is against their own national interests and the interests of world stability."

What is most interesting about Reston's article is his argument that when a nation goes its own way in international affairs, it is because of "disenchantment and even bitterness about the cost and complexity of world affairs"—and, in the case of the United States, a sign of "weariness and resentment at the price of American leadership."

An opposite point of view will be taken here: shibboleths such as "delicate balance of power in the world" are symptomatic of what the 19th century Englishman, Walter Bagehot, called "easy ideas" in

---

[1] "The Angry Hangover," *New York Times* (October 29, 1971).

politics. Such ideas provide labels for highly complicated fields of political action, but the stark imagery of these labels evokes a picture of the world that oversimplifies.[2] Terms such as "leadership" and "balance of power" are expressions of national transcendence *over* world affairs and not of national involvement *within* the field of conflicting policies; such transcendence or paramountcy is illusory because it proves fleeting or nonexistent. Hence, just as the new policy toward the People's Republic of China represents an independent American appraisal of the world that breaks old shibboleths about the "delicate balance of power" that previous presidents once used to exclude Peking from the U.N., so this same independence allows for experimentation with a "two Chinas" policy in the U.N. The contradictory aspects of this approach express the complexity of foreign policy, not an escape from that complexity. Such contradictions are, perhaps, reliable indicators of real experience, whereas efforts to resolve contradictions through analytical devices, such as the idea of a delicate power in the world, may not be realistic.

Recognition of complexity in international policy may require the jettisoning of easy ideas in favor of more ambiguous, but realistic, symbols. In place of such masterful evocative images as balance of power, political complexity may have to be recognized as a tangled field of reasons, decisions, policies, results and assessments where actors do not have the privilege of transcendence over this field. At most, horizons can be seen but there is, as yet, no map; leaders become explorers rather than demigods. Here asymmetry among policies and disjunction between events are commonplace, old shibboleths lose their power, and new opportunities beckon. A heightened sense of opportunities amidst events, due to contradictions in the field of action, pushes national policy in new and independent directions. This new experience of complexity, infinitely more labyrinthine in symbolic expression than the imagery of "balance" can suggest, may well be the foundation of President Nixon's revised policy toward the People's Republic of China.

Surely this kind of complexity provided the experience for those who worked closely on American Middle East policy during that most eventful year, 1970. Such was the pace of events that the only course of action open for the United States was one of initiative and independence from the old shibboleths of global balance that some would

---

[2] See the discussion of political symbolization, including Bagehot's arguments in *The English Constitution*, contained in Pranger, *Action, Symbolism, and Order*, Chapter V.

like to apply to all situations where the United States and the U.S.S.R. are rivals. A backward look at the chronology of major events in the Middle East during 1970, especially in the period from early January until late September, provides a dizzying experience. One can only imagine the sensation of those closely involved with these events, as they unfolded, in the Department of State, the Department of Defense, the National Security Council staff and the Central Intelligence Agency. Some events were direct outcomes of United States decisions, but the full chronology was much broader and thus quite independent of American policy at certain points.

In January, Israel launched its deep penetration raids into Egypt with Phantom jets and other aircraft; by the end of the month, rumors, which were denied by Cairo, told of a secret visit to Moscow by President Nasser. In early February, an important Arab summit meeting spared the United States a total rupture of its remaining relations with the Arabs—in spite of earlier signs that stiff Arab retaliation would follow the first deliveries of F-4s to Israel in the last quarter of 1969.

During March, the U.S.S.R. installed a new surface-to-air missile system in Egypt, embracing both SAM-2 and SAM-3 capabilities. In addition, reports circulated telling of increased numbers of Soviet personnel manning these missile sites and the central command-and-control facilities for the system, as well as Russian-manned aircraft to protect these personnel. Also, the United States deferred its long-awaited decision on sale of additional F-4s to Israel. During April, Assistant Secretary of State Joseph Sisco toured the Middle East, but was forced to cancel his visit to Jordan when Palestinian protests threatened anarchy in Amman.

Beginning in May and continuing until late July, Israel began its intensive air strikes against Egyptian positions along the Suez Canal. On May 1, President Nasser warned the United States, in unambiguous language, that further sale of Phantom jets to Israel would spell the end of American interests in the Arab Middle East. Exactly one month later, more than two-thirds of the United States Senate sponsored a petition to President Nixon calling for the sale of more Phantoms to Israel. Late in the same month, however, the United States presented a new peace plan to the U.S.S.R., to the Arabs and to Israel—a plan calling, among other things, for a cease-fire of limited duration. Just two months after Nasser's warning and amidst daily stories of grisly warfare between Israel and Egypt, President Nixon likened the Middle East in 1970 to the Balkans before World War I, a very dangerous spot that threatened to pull the U.S. and

U.S.S.R. into direct war. During July, reports circulated of Egyptian SAM-2 and SAM-3 batteries close to the Suez Canal, and for the first time Israel suffered multiple losses of F-4s in that area.

In late July, however, the U.A.R., Jordan and Israel accepted the terms of the American 90-day cease-fire proposal, a proposal with potentially great consequences for peace in the Middle East (the truce was extended in November 1970, then allowed to lapse in 1971 but with no resumption of warfare). The acceptance was greeted by popular enthusiasm in Egypt and Israel, but scorned by the Palestinian leadership in Jordan who threatened, and then precipitated in September, civil war against King Hussein. As if to dramatize the serious state of events just prior to the cease-fire, Hedrick Smith published a long article in the *New York Times* of July 17 reporting that Israel possessed nuclear weapons, a story categorically denied by Israel the following day. On the day of Israel's formal acceptance of the cease-fire, August 4, it was reported that several Russian pilots flying Egyptian aircraft had been shot down by the Israeli Air Force, a report confirmed by Israel on October 26.

From August until late in the year, the air was alive with Israel's charges that the U.A.R. was violating the cease-fire's "standstill" provisions by moving additional surface-to-air missiles into the 50-kilometer standstill zone. (These charges were finally confirmed by the United States during the first week of September.) Also, from August until late 1970 Ambassador Gunnar Jarring attempted to move peace negotiations forward, but his efforts were boycotted by Israel until December 18 in reaction to Egyptian violations of the cease-fire.

September proved to be one of the most momentous months in modern Middle Eastern history. A Palestinian left-wing group, the Popular Front for the Liberation of Palestine (PFLP), hijacked four jet airliners, forcing three of them to land on Jordan's remote Dawson airstrip, holding the passengers hostage, and then demolishing the planes. Also, the Palestinians made good their threat to initiate civil war in Jordan; assisted by Syria's active intervention, they collided with the Jordan Arab Army during the last half of September. Jordan repulsed the Syrians and broke the back of the Palestine commando or *"fedayeen"* insurgency. The month ended with President Nasser's sudden death on September 28. After a short period of drift, Egypt named Anwar Sadat as Nasser's successor.

Five key American decisions, each of them analyzed here, were made during this remarkably fluid period for international relations in the Middle East. They are the decisions to (1) defer a final decision on the sale of additional F-4s and A-4s to Israel (March 23), (2) sponsor, with guarantees to Israel, a cease-fire for 90 days (publicly proposed on June 25, accepted in late July by the combatants), (3) confirm Egyptian breaches of the cease-fire (early September), (4) give active encouragement to the resumption of Arab-Israeli peace talks through Jarring's mediation, and (5) take an active role, on Jordan's behalf, in its efforts against Syrian intervention during the civil strife of September.

The Politics of Military Assistance:
Israel's Second Request for F-4 Phantom Jets

In the wake of the first deliveries of Phantom jets to Israel in late 1969, fulfilling President Johnson's 1968 decision to sell such aircraft, a second increment of F-4s plus additional A-4 Skyhawks was requested by Israel in the fall of 1969.[3] News of this request spread rapidly and became a *cause célèbre* in the Middle East and within the United States government until well into 1971 when the government of Israel stated publicly it would no longer cooperate with American peace initiatives until it received more jets.[4] For Arabs, the supersonic Phantom jet was a symbol of powerful American support for Israel against the Arab world; for Israelis, the aircraft had deep emotional significance, representing Israel's reluctant but necessary reliance on the United States as its only great power patron. During 1969 the Arabs basked in Soviet largesse, enjoyed Anglo-French favor, and received some American military assistance (Jordan, Lebanon, Saudi Arabia in the Eastern Mediterranean), but Israel was threatened by Russian military forces and officially snubbed on arms assistance in London and Paris. Israeli-flown French fighter bombers had destroyed Egypt's air force in 1967; and it was to the French primarily and Americans only secondarily (through subsonic Skyhawk purchases negotiated in the mid-1960s) that Israel first turned to modernize its aging air force, with 50 Mirage V fighters as the central focus. However, impressed by the proven performance of the F-4 in Vietnam, the Israelis approached President Johnson in 1968 and obtained his approval for an initial sale.[5] This was an important

---

[3] Publicly confirmed by Secretary Rogers, on March 23, 1970, to be 25 F-4s and 100 A-4s (*New York Times*, March 24, 1970).

[4] See Prime Minister Meir's speech to the Knesset of October 26, 1971, in *New York Times* (October 27, 1971).

[5] With its supersonic speed at high and low altitudes, its great range, and its impressive ordnance capacity, the F-4 is probably one of the most formidable warplanes ever built.

victory for Israel, because its air force had been denied the Mirage Vs when President de Gaulle, in the wake of the 1967 war, placed an embargo on major lethal end-items scheduled for Israel. After Israel's commando raid on the Beirut airport, December 28, 1968, the embargo was extended to cover even spare parts.

Unfortunately for Israel, its second request for F-4s and A-4s in late 1969 coincided with plans for a major American diplomatic offensive in the Middle East, aimed in part at recouping American losses in the Arab world incurred after June 1967. That such losses benefited the Soviet Union more than the Arabs was appreciated in Washington and in key Arab capitals still friendly to the United States (most notably Amman, Beirut and Riyadh). From the Israeli standpoint, however, a narrower perspective was taken: steady erosion of United States influence in various Arab states, particularly in Egypt, was thought to represent a gain for Israel's security interests, because American policy would now have to adjust to what friends it had left in the Eastern Mediterranean. Also, the Israelis did not believe, at this time, that the U.S.S.R. would benefit much from its newly found preeminence in Egypt and other leftist Arab nations.

Two such different views of where American policy ought to head in 1969 were bound to create friction between the United States and Israel over options for the future. This clash of interests suffused the diplomatic dialogue concerning additional Phantoms. It was strongly argued in the United States government—and this view prevailed—that to survive in the Middle East in its rivalry with the U.S.S.R., a rivalry that still seemed of great interest to the Soviet Union in late 1969, the United States would have to devise a policy that was balanced in two respects: externally, favors would have to be bestowed or denied to the Arabs and Israel with a certain neutrality; and internally, the policy would have to balance long-term principles with short-term maneuver. So complicated was the policy field, however, that principles could not be completely reconciled (Israel's security versus Arab friendship were not totally contradictory but neither were they very symmetrical, especially in Arab and Israeli eyes); maneuvers were at variance (the timing of the second Phantom request versus the timing of new overtures to the Arabs); and principles and maneuvers could not always be aligned. These contradictions were never brought into a monolithic policy, the most feasible approach being a policy without homogeneous structure. From the Israeli perspective, the contradiction between principles and maneuvers was the most important; what the United States saw as a problem of timing and maneuver in the Israeli Phantom case, the government of Israel saw as a matter of principle for its own security. Those who tried to raise the issue for the United States to the level of principle, by arguing that supply of such aircraft clashed with American national interests, found the conflict even more intense. And, of course, some urged further supply as a matter of principle for United States policy.

The "interim" decision by the United States government in March 1970, namely, to delay a final answer on the Phantoms pending outcome of new peace initiatives, chose the lesser of two evils: recognizing that further supply of Phantoms to Israel in the spring of 1970 would cause severe dislocation of American interests in the Middle East, but also recognizing that Israel's acquiescence to American peace plans remained essential for those plans to work, the decision *to delay* a final decision on the second increment of Phantoms made the American position one of maneuver rather than principle. Hence the conflict between the United States and Israel over this request, and Israel's disappointment with the outcome, did not reach the level of such profound differences of principle that *both* sides took ideological positions. Israel, which held to a principled position on its security and would brook no compromise on the necessity for having more Phantoms (whatever the American studies on military balance might indicate), could nevertheless rely on the American position as one of tactical maneuver, not hard-and-fast principle against further supply of Phantom aircraft. Here the conflict between the United States and Israel on American policy toward the Arab world was evident, but the United States chose to keep the military supply question—so emotional for Israel—in the area of maneuver and *not* to equate such supply with its long-term interests in improving relations with the Arabs. That the two issues were interrelated was self-evident; that they were identical could not be argued, for it would have spelled the end of American influence with the most powerful military force in the Middle East, Israel. Having no other great power to turn to, Israel could find itself backed into a corner, a very dangerous situation for the Middle East and the world. American maneuvers in the Middle East have focused on preventing any of the combatants from judging the field of forces to be so confused that it would take drastic action: under these circumstances, anxieties lying close to the surface would become manifest. In Israel's case, they would be nameless anxieties about annihilation, in the Arab case, equally powerful anxieties about vitality of culture and personality in the mid-20th century.

The Arabs, of course, wished to treat American military supplies to Israel as a matter of principle not maneuver, at least until prospects for peace brightened in mid-1970, because the Phantom aircraft threatened their military security. Here superior Israeli military abilities raised again, as they have ever since Israel's independence, Arab anxieties over coping with modernity. And no nation, so worried, can treat its own security as a matter for maneuver and compromise. Hence in 1970 the United States informed the Arabs that the decision to delay a final verdict on the Israeli request was an "interim" decision only, thus alerting Arab capitals that the military supply issue was *not* a fundamental question in the mind of the United States in the sense that its national interests were identified exclusively with Israel or wholly with the Arabs. Furthermore, the Arabs should know, it was observed, that since the U.S.S.R. *had* made its military supply of Arab forces a matter of principle as well as maneuver, breaking relations with Israel in 1967 and in other ways leading a confrontation against Israel since, there were dangers that Arab independence might become jeopardized. For if each state must treat its own military security as a paramount principle, then superpowers who come to identify their security interests as identical with those of lesser states also threaten the autonomy of such states to determine their own security policy. Then one can speak of a large power "pressuring" a smaller power by using military assistance as a lever to move that power into line behind the greater power's interests.

Some believe, of course, that military assistance should always operate as such a lever. However, this view overestimates the power of assistance, in itself, to influence directly another nation's foreign policy, and it also underestimates the symbolic value of such assistance as an element in tactical maneuver and timing. Basically, however, the idea that such assistance is a "tool" rather than a "tactic" or "gambit" provides yet another example of using linear, mechanical and behavioral images of stimulus and response, cause and effect, for events in a tangled policy field where causation is so contingent that these images become irrelevant.[6]

In announcing the American interim decision on March 23, 1970, Secretary of State Rogers linked it to new "serious initiatives" by the United States to end the Middle East conflict, particularly efforts

---

[6] For an interesting discussion of this, see Geoffrey Kemp, *Arms and Security: The Egypt-Israel Case*, Adelphi Paper No. 52 (London: Institute for Strategic Studies, October 1968).

to secure a cease-fire between Israel and its Arab neighbors.[7] Also, both sides were asked to reappraise their maximal, hardline positions in order to clear a way for new negotiation efforts by Ambassador Jarring. Finally, with a gesture toward principles, the secretary at once referred to the necessity for carrying out Security Council Resolution 242 of 1967 (so important for the Arabs) and also for sustaining Israel's security under the concept of "balance." The idea of balance had by now become a watchword for United States policy in the Middle East, denoting American support for the principles of Israel's security and for United Nations resolutions, and yet at the same time connoting an element of maneuver and timing in American arms supply policy toward Israel.

During 1970 and 1971 Israel has continued to press for an American policy that would guarantee an uninterrupted flow of jet warplanes and other material, while the United States has generally relied on maneuver in its military supply relationships with Israel. Such maneuvering is impressive to Israel, and thus instrumental in securing Israel's acceptance of American peace plans, only as long as initiatives toward peace actually produce results perceptible to Israel—in which case the delay appears to Jerusalem as purely tactical and, in the absence of escalating warfare, disappointing but not unacceptable. If results can no longer be expected from initiatives or if these results prove uninteresting for the inertial forces of national security—and here powerful Israel can fulfill its own pessimistic forecast about peace prospects by simply refusing to cooperate—then the delay in military supplies is interpreted by Israel as a matter of principle in American policy. When this perception occurs, even if the United States does not actually intend it, then it *appears* that the United States is "pressuring" Israel into a peace settlement by withholding the aircraft.

As American initiatives slowed down in 1971, partly because of Israeli truculence but also for reasons connected with other actors (each actor blamed the others), Israel began complaining that the United States was using the F-4 delays as a matter of principle rather than maneuver. Those who rely on military assistance as a pressure point, and see such pressure as maneuver, can achieve results through such a policy only as long as those being pressured play the same game and accept the delay as maneuver. But since political action moves as much by appearance as design, tactical pressure deliberately designed by one power can rapidly turn into a battle of principles

---

[7] *New York Times* (March 23, 1970).

when so *perceived* by the other power. Again, the fluidity of the policy field makes itself apparent.

Cease-fire of August 1970

Caught between the Arab demand for deeds as well as words and the Israeli belief that only real signs of a settlement could justify the United States using matters of Israel's security for maneuver, the decision to treat Israel's second request for Phantoms and Skyhawks as a tactical issue was daring. If this choice had not been coupled with signs that new initiatives were underway, however, it would have appeared to be either a matter of principle that no more Phantoms would be sold to Israel or that the United States was indulging in maneuver for want of policy. Hence the March interim decision effectively combined principle, maneuver and timing, but as a holding action at best. Such an action without new peace initiatives in the offing would have poisoned American relations with Israel at a time when the United States needed Israeli acquiescence, which it seemingly could not force, in order to achieve peace in the Middle East.

The new initiative was first proposed privately on June 19, and then announced publicly by Secretary Rogers on June 25. He stated that whereas the earlier decision on Phantom jets had been necessary to hold a way open for productive negotiations on peace, the principle of peace was now paramount in a new American plan: he urged the parties "to stop shooting and start talking." In addition, he noted that the military supply channel to Israel would best be kept as submerged as possible in the hope that public attention might be focused on diplomatic activity. Instead of announcing, as some observers expected he would, the sale of Phantoms to Israel without necessarily giving the numbers (there was a lot of speculation about numbers too), the secretary buried the issue under an initiative for a cease-fire and indirect talks under Jarring. Only the cease-fire proposal was new, a step beyond the plan presented in the secretary's address to the Galaxy Conference on December 9, 1969.[8]

Egypt had already indicated a willingness to accept a temporary cease-fire before the Rogers press conference of June 26. In fact, in some circles, the public announcement of the initiative was thought to be an answer to President Nasser's May 1 appeal to President Nixon that the United States reevaluate its Middle East policy before it was too late (in that speech the Egyptian leader had referred to

---

[8] *New York Times* (June 26, 1970).

a letter he had sent President Nixon). Whatever the impulse for this public announcement of a new initiative—and it was surely also, in part, because the United States had promised in March that within three months it would give a verdict on more Phantoms for Israel—important spade work was required in order to convince Israel and Jordan that a cease-fire was in their interest. Jordan would seemingly follow Egypt's lead in accepting the temporary truce, but King Hussein would have to weigh his acceptance against *fedayeen* threats to create severe problems for his government if he accepted. On the other hand, although Israel had indicated considerable flexibility on its demand for direct negotiations with the Arabs, just as Egypt had proved amenable to moderating its demand for total Israeli withdrawal *before* negotiations (neither power had given up these positions as ultimate demands, however), Israel was then rejecting the idea of a limited cease-fire and remaining noncommittal on the issue of when and where it would withdraw.

During the next month, under extremely adverse conditions of intense warfare along the Suez Canal, negotiations toward a cease-fire took place directly between the United States on the one hand and Egypt, Israel and Jordan on the other. Late in July, first Egypt and then Jordan and Israel agreed to terms jointly sponsored by the United States and the U.S.S.R.: all fighting would cease for 90 days and military activity in a 50-kilometer wide zone on both sides of the Suez Canal would come to a complete standstill. In turn, the United States and U.S.S.R. would guarantee to the parties and to each other observance of the cease-fire's terms. Ambassador Jarring would immediately undertake a new mission of mediation. On August 8 the cease-fire went into effect amidst hopes expressed in Washington, Moscow, Amman, Cairo and Jerusalem that it would open new avenues for peace in the Middle East. Except for the Palestinian Resistance Movement and for Syria and Iraq—who refused to ratify the cease-fire (their resistance was to prove fateful in the following month)—public opinion in the region appeared relieved to learn that war was temporarily ended. It remained to be seen, however, whether any of the chief actors in the policy field could adjust their policies sufficiently to sustain the American initiative into even more effective steps toward a major breakthrough.

The cease-fire plan tapped an important inertial force, the spasmodic nature of war in the region. This factor reflects the inability of either Israel or the Arabs to wage protracted total war. States with fragile GNPs, who are already devoting a disproportionate share of their resources not just to defense but to actual warfare, cannot sustain wars of attrition. Furthermore, the economies of these states are maintained by trained manpower that cannot be lost in warfare without adverse consequences for these economies. Finally, the armies are basically oriented toward private, not public, life: Israel relies on citizen-soldiers called up from reserve for the bulk of its total armed force; Egypt and Jordan depend upon a manpower base that finds the idea of a "nation-at-war," which is the concept of total war, alien. When he began his attritive campaign against Israel, President Nasser no doubt calculated all these factors as working against Israel. As usual, he overestimated his own country's stamina and underestimated Israel's.

Without unlimited superpower patronage, neither Israel nor any Arab state can continue intense warfare over a long duration. For its part, whereas the U.S.S.R. surely saw advantages to rivalry with the United States, it must also have seen that the United States had only delayed its decision on more Phantoms. Hence the dangers to the U.S.S.R. of becoming involved as a partner in total war with Egypt must have been weighed by Moscow against the opportunities that such a partnership would offer. In the end, both the United States and the Soviet Union, probably for quite different reasons, stopped short of such partnerships, and the parties in conflict grew weary. The cease-fire exploited this weariness to the mutual benefit of all.

The cease-fire's success provides an object lesson for all further steps toward real peace in the Middle East: each phase must be designed, not only to follow after the previous one in a logical way, but to tap the underlying inertial forces at work in the policy field in such a manner that each party's self-interest, for different reasons, accepts the step. Also, as such steps accumulate—and it seemed to some in August 1970, and to even more later, that opening the Suez Canal should be the step following the cease-fire—it is important that all parties not only look backward in satisfaction but also look forward in anticipation of what future steps will entail. The recommendations at the end of this study attempt to do this, beginning with the cease-fire and the opening of Suez.

Curiously, the American decisions ancillary to the cease-fire brought the United States directly into a war of words with Israel, the U.A.R. and the U.S.S.R. At the same time, the United States gave the negotiator's task, which it had so ably undertaken, back to Ambassador Jarring. Having brought about the cease-fire through a combination of inspired principle and patient maneuver, the United States dropped principle and maneuver to concentrate its attention on the crises of August and September. What should have been a U.N. function, to supervise the cease-fire with special support from the United States (e.g., helicopters), was assumed instead by the United States and the U.S.S.R. with their own national systems of surveillance. On the other hand, the United States efforts at a cease-fire, which seemed to dictate additional American efforts after August 8, were spent in encouraging a Jarring mission that quickly became embroiled in the missile violation controversy that followed August 8. Paradoxically, while American plans have always featured Ambassador Jarring as the chief mediator between the Arabs and Israelis, the successes wrought by these plans have come from the active efforts by the United States directly with the parties involved. The cease-fire was achieved this way and, with American stock soaring in the Middle East after August 8, there was every reason to believe that the United States could strike again with yet more steps, such as immediate opening of the Suez Canal. Instead, the United States government became transfixed, first by the hopeless argument over Egyptian violations of the cease-fire's standstill provisions and then by the Jordan crisis of September. The result was that the impetus present on August 8 began to evaporate, and has not yet been restored.

Cease-fire Violations

Having disentangled enough of the web of Middle East policy interests to bring about a cease-fire, the United States was faced with a hard future. On the one hand, the cease-fire provided the most auspicious sign of change since at least the 1967 war and perhaps even before, because no war had left the bitterness that this one had. But on the other hand, only part of the web had been untangled. As noted at the beginning of this essay, the inertial forces in the Middle East consist of tenacious peoples, ancient memories, modern aspirations and spasmodic wars. If these forces are to be used in a search for peace, they need harnessing. The war had ended on August 8, at least temporarily, because American policy had capitalized on the weariness of Arabs and Israelis. But the hurdle of historical memories would prove more difficult to cross: past truces between Israel and the Arabs had been characterized by constant violations and inadequate policing from United Nations supervisory forces. The Israelis, remembering the sudden withdrawal of U.N. forces from the Sinai in 1967, were particularly sensitive to the U.N.'s past inadequacies.

The question of just who should police the cease-fire was, therefore, a critical question. The American proposal assigned supervision to the parties themselves, with support from the United States and U.S.S.R., rather than to United Nations forces. True, about 100 U.N. observers would be stationed at Qantara, Egypt, but they were to assist, not to operate, surveillance. This solved the problem of Israeli suspicion of U.N. truce supervision, but it did not reach the heart of the matter: United Nations forces had experienced difficulties in the past because Arab-Israeli hostilities continued after the cease-fire and not because United Nations forces were present. Under the new truce, the United States would become a guarantor of the cease-fire, but in the process would place itself in a position of mediator between Arabs and Israelis—*on this one question but not on the wider terms of settlement*—who had a long history of truce violations. Actually, this decision could have taken one of two directions: to use the United Nations and lend it extra support; or to substitute an American guarantee coupled with national means of surveillance and U.N. reporting procedures. If the first course had been chosen, violations would have become truly international in significance, instead of being confined within a four-cornered dispute involving Israel, the U.A.R., U.S.S.R. and United States. Under the cease-fire's terms, the parties would use their own means of surveillance but only report violations to the United Nations.

Prime Minister Meir's government had survived the withdrawal of hard-line Gahal members from the cabinet over Israel's acceptance of the cease-fire. It now faced the strong possibility that Egypt, out of military necessity more than political chicanery, would continue to complete and to shift its missile launcher positions within the 50-kilometer standstill zone in anticipation of a surprise Israeli attack. After all, not only would the United States fly reconnaissance missions over the canal, but so would Egypt and Israel. That Egypt expected new warfare and that Israel was probably alert to this Egyptian expectation are both indicative of the vicious circles-within-circles so characteristic of the Middle East policy field. Sound military doctrine dictates the use of "worst case" examples in planning a defense; and since all critical relationships between Israel and Egypt after 1947 had been military ones, it seemed only logical (some might call it irrational) to treat every encounter—no matter how innocuous—as a worst case situation. This logic appeared all the more compelling because of the propensity of both sides to treat their conflict as a war of political ideas, and hence a struggle between self-fulfilling ideologies, as well as battle between armed forces.[9] That Egypt went even beyond such movements to augment its missile capabilities was reported by Israel in complaints filed with the United Nations. In turn, the U.A.R. charged that Israel was also violating the truce. Reports of violations on both sides were confirmed by the United States, but the major American effort was spent in verifying and supporting Israeli charges of Egyptian violations. As it turned out, this effort proved neither comforting to Israel nor reassuring to the Arabs.

To police the cease-fire, the United States employed U-2 aircraft. Having decided to use such means, however, Washington became the target of angry accusations from Israel (it was not doing enough) and from the U.A.R. (it was doing too much), both of whom were also deploying their own reconnaissance aircraft to check each other's movements, as well as to anticipate and double-check American findings. Confusion was bound to develop where the United States, Egypt, Israel and presumably the U.S.S.R. all undertook sophisticated aerial photography, especially when Israel and Egypt kept daily, suspicious track of each other for military reasons.

As early as August 13, five days after the truce began, Israel charged that the U.A.R. had violated the standstill agreement. Predictably, Egypt filed countercharges. Prime Minister Meir noted on August 31 that her country was "now in the midst of a hard, difficult argument with the United States over Egyptian violations of the cease-fire," thus bringing to public attention the private debate taking place between the two countries. She cited the American guarantee that neither side would improve its military position during the truce. On September 3, the same day that the United States officially confirmed Israel's charges, Israel asked the United States to seek missile removal by the U.A.R. Washington turned to Cairo the next day and asked for Egyptian "rectification" of their violations, a request heatedly rejected by the U.A.R. who was supported by the Soviet Union. The United States was "undermining" the cease-fire, said Egypt on September 10; four days later Egyptian Foreign Minister Riad accused the United States of yielding to Israeli pressure in making "baseless accusations" against the U.A.R.; and on the following day Riad declared the American peace initiative "dead" because

---

[9] This generalization is not meant to slight those in the Middle East who refuse to participate in these vicious circles or who do so for tactical reasons only. Indeed, without such persons in key positions, peace would be impossible. The chronology that follows is based on *Facts on File*, Vol. XXX (1970).

of new economic and military assistance for Israel. Egypt would, however, continue to observe the cease-fire. Riad's last declaration was accompanied, on the same day, by an American charge that Israel too had violated the standstill agreement (denied by Israel). Mrs. Meir announced on September 18 that Israel would keep the truce, but would not talk peace until Egyptian missiles were removed, thus, in effect, short-circuiting the Jarring mission then at work in Arab capitals. After asking for restoration of the truce's integrity on September 30, the United States said on October 6 that it wanted to suspend the Big Four talks on peace pending Egyptian rectification. Between October 8 and 10, the United States and U.S.S.R. exchanged charges about the violations. On October 26, the United States reconfirmed Israel's reports and, on the following day, claimed that the U.A.R. had tacitly admitted breaches. In the last days of October, Israel and the U.S.S.R. traded polemics in the United Nations on this subject. By mid-November, Egypt's Anwar Sadat was predicting war's renewal, in the context of a generally tough line by Cairo on extending the cease-fire beyond its second 90-day period. However, Israel dropped its demand for pullback of Egyptian missiles on November 18, and announced one month later that it would rejoin the Jarring talks. (By then Jarring had returned to his permanent post as Swedish ambassador to the U.S.S.R.) As if to underscore the fact that both Egypt and Israel were poised for immediate resumption of warfare, an Israeli patrol boat sank an Egyptian motor launch off the Sinai coast in the Gulf of Suez on November 28. On the same day, Egypt's *Al-Ahram* reported that the Egyptian government would protest American U-2 flights because they were merely spying on Egyptian positions; it also charged that, by its new assistance to Israel, the United States had "nullified" the truce. The United States, in turn, expressed surprise that Egypt and the U.S.S.R. did not know such flights were taking place and stated that they had been terminated on November 10.

Any renewal of the cease-fire might well have been imperiled by these developments, but the United Nations General Assembly voted a 90-day extension on November 4, a resolution supported by the U.A.R. but opposed by the United States and Israel because it did not provide for Egyptian rectification of its violations. Fighting did not resume. Perhaps as significant was the report that, in a November 22 cabinet meeting, Defense Minister Dayan had proposed a long-term truce with Egypt based on mutual withdrawal of heavy weapons from the Suez Canal area and the opening of the waterway to international traffic. This rumor was never confirmed by official

Israeli sources. In any event after it surfaced, an increasing amount of public interest began to focus on the step *after* the cease-fire, with the clearing of the Suez Canal as a possible phase two in an overall settlement. This interest grew in 1971 with the new Egyptian proposals of early February.

Other things being equal, the United States should never have involved itself, by certain initial choices it made, in the business of answering charges and insinuations that were bound to arise after the cease-fire's start. By becoming a guarantor and by relinquishing active negotiations on further steps toward peace to Ambassador Jarring, even though it had negotiated the cease-fire, the United States became preoccupied and lost momentum toward a more comprehensive settlement. Jarring himself could not talk with Israel—because Jerusalem would not talk with him until the United States could obtain rectification of the violations, a rectification Washington could not deliver. But because the United Nations was directly involved in the dispute solely as a reporting organization with no independent powers of surveillance, it could do nothing but urge the parties to continue negotiations under Jarring. The peacemaking roles of supervision and negotiation should have all been held by the United Nations, *or* all by the United States, *or* split in such a way that the inevitable contention of ancient memories about truce violations would continue to be absorbed by the United Nations as it had been in the past. It was no place for the United States to be directly involved, to say nothing of offering its guarantees.

There is, perhaps, a simple lesson here for those who propose that the United States should actively provide unilateral guarantees for Israel's territorial security in the event of a peace settlement. Is any single outside power really capable of mastering the complexities of Arab-Israeli relations sufficiently to take on such a task? [10] What would be the consequences of using an outside nation's armed forces in a situation as filled with ambiguity and half-truth as this one? Is such a break with traditional United Nations arrangements really necessary, or can U.N. peacekeeping, both in theory and practice, be strengthened? Can American military ingenuity be applied to making multilateral peacekeeping efforts work better? Significantly, on De-

---

[10] For example, in his December 23 interview with James Reston of the *New York Times*, President Sadat said that even if Egypt did reach a peace settlement with Israel, it would still not begin formal diplomatic relations with Israel during his lifetime. Hence, a guarantor power would be forced into an intermediary role, even after a peace settlement!

cember 23, Secretary Rogers told a news conference that the United States had "not excluded the possibility" of participating in a United Nations peacekeeping force as an added assurance that a peace settlement between Israel and the Arabs would be observed.

It is possible, however, that any of the above three alternatives pertaining to supervision and negotiation would have proved unacceptable to Israel or the Arabs. The arrangement that developed *was* acceptable. Furthermore, the cease-fire has held up over time, even though no further steps have been taken toward peace and despite the absence of formal renewal after the second 90-day extension in late 1970. And, of course, the missile violation crisis did pass. On the other hand, it may turn out that, in the process of the crisis, the cease-fire metamorphosed from a step toward peace into a breathing spell between wars. Perhaps no arrangement could have prevented this. Nevertheless, Israel may have become further disenchanted by American "guarantees" of its security interests; Egypt may have concluded that the United States would back Israel in a hard peace, just as it had in a bitter war; and the U.S.S.R. may have come to the dangerous conclusion that its counsel with Egypt, no matter how disruptive of American plans, would prevail.

Surely the various alternatives for supervision and negotiation were worth a closer look by the United States and other actors before the cease-fire went into effect. As a world organization subject to the stresses of competing national interests, the United Nations is expected to have difficulties enforcing its guarantees; this expectation has become almost institutionalized in its truce supervision machinery in the Middle East. But an unfulfilled American guarantee can lead to serious problems of national credibility that may blunt future peace efforts in the Middle East. Was it really necessary for the United States to expend so much credibility in order to obtain this cease-fire? The maneuver was successful, the principle dubious. Fortunately, the United States finally gave up efforts to police the standstill zone on November 10, leaving Israel and Egypt to their own resources.

Time had been lost and momentum dissipated in the missile crisis, a deceleration made all the more rapid by events in Jordan during September. Additional phases should have followed quickly after August 8 in order to prevent the cleared roads from becoming congested again, and to provide new instruments for disentangling other paths to peace. But the only indication of further thinking from August until the end of 1970 were the rumors about Dayan's position and Secretary Rogers' reference to a possible American role in a U.N. peacekeeping force at his news conference of December 23.

By year's end, in separate interviews with the *New York Times* columnist, James Reston, on December 19 and 23 respectively, Prime Minister Meir and President Sadat expressed ritualized pessimism about peace in the near future, if at all. In the course of his interview, Sadat laid down, for the first time publicly, Egyptian terms for peace with Israel: his precondition that Israel must withdraw from "every inch" of Egyptian territory occupied in 1967 before peace could be made, was bound to fulfill Mrs. Meir's prediction (or prophecy) of four days earlier that the Egyptians "are not going to accept what we want, nor are we prepared to accept what they want after two or three sessions." [11] Perhaps it was merely a casual slip-of-tongue that President Sadat had reversed the terms of his predecessor's acceptance of the cease-fire in July 1970: what had been, according to the BBC Monitoring Service, President Nasser's position that Israel would withdraw *after* implementation of the Security Council's 1967 resolution for a "just and permanent peace" recognizing the territorial integrity of all states had reverted, in late December 1970, to the harder line that *first* Israel must withdraw from every inch of territory and *then* Cairo would recognize Israel under the terms of the Security Council resolution.[12] Had the dialectical terms of withdrawal and peace been reversed to their earlier, insoluble relationship? Only time would tell.

The Jarring Mission, August to November 1970

Probably no single individual worked so diligently for peace in the Middle East after the Six-Day War of 1967 as did Sweden's ambassador to the U.S.S.R., Gunnar Jarring. From November 23, 1967 when United Nations Secretary General U Thant appointed the ambassador his special envoy to the Middle East, Jarring shuttled tirelessly between the Arabs and Israel in an effort to move the terms of Security Council Resolution 242 forward to a peace settlement. From the start he ran into the inertia of warfare between the combatants. Israel agreed to talks with the Arabs at Cyprus, under Jarring's auspices, but the U.A.R. bitterly rejected the plan because Israel refused to promise to withdraw from all Arab lands occupied in the 1967 war before talks would begin. Throughout 1968 and 1969, the dialectics of peace and withdrawal plagued Jarring's mission: the Arabs insisting that Israel withdraw before talks began, the Israelis arguing that the Arabs

---

[11] *Facts on File*, Vol. XXX (1970), pp. 949C-2-950A-2.
[12] Compare *Facts on File*, Vol. XXX (1970), p. 529D-1, with *ibid.*, p. 950B-1.

should start talking first. In an effort to break this impasse, talks were held between the U.S. and U.S.S.R. and among the Big Four in 1969, but with vigorous opposition from Israel who suspected that a settlement plan would be imposed that might provide the Arabs with an escape from negotiations for a peace treaty.

Having urged the resumption of peace talks under Jarring as part of the Rogers Plan of December 1969, the United States pushed for a relaunching of Jarring's mission in its June 25, 1970 proposal for the parties "to stop shooting and start talking." Surely no one possessed Ambassador Jarring's experience in this most difficult area of mediating the peace-and-withdrawal issue, but no one had experienced so much frustration either. It was significant that in his acceptance of the American proposal for a cease-fire on July 23, President Nasser publicly supported the idea of reaching an agreement on a just peace first and *then* expediting Israel's withdrawal from the territories occupied in 1967, an apparent softening of Egypt's standard position that unconditional withdrawal must precede peace. Similarly, Israel's acceptance on July 31 included the statement that "no prior conditions" would be interposed by Israel in resumption of talks under Jarring (which, of course, meant the same for Israel's enemies). In other words, the chief antagonists had accepted both the cease-fire and peace talks unconditionally. The United States had every reason to believe, therefore, that signs augured well for Jarring's success in his new round of negotiations.

Unfortunately, the abrupt and somewhat startling transformation of the Middle East from warfare to truce left unsettled Israel's concern over the new SAM-2 and SAM-3 system that Egypt was installing, with Soviet assistance, in the zone immediately adjacent to the Suez Canal. For this reason, the importance of the standstill provision in the cease-fire was underscored by President Nixon in his statement of July 31 expressing gratification over Israel's acceptance. It was on this rock that Jarring's new mission broke apart, as charges and countercharges were traded during late 1970, and Israel refused to participate in peace talks.

Yet perhaps there was another, more symbolic reason for Jarring's lack of success in 1970. It was clear in his earlier efforts that the combatants were variously unhappy with his proposals. His missions were associated with the deadlocked, dialectical struggle over whether peace would come before withdrawal or vice versa. He possessed no special persuasiveness, such as a representative from a great power might have, in dealing with this intractable situation. Furthermore, he did not have the resources for reassessing the situation, coming to new conclusions and formulating creative policies, such as a nation like the United States can muster when its basic national interests are at stake. Hence the Middle East was transfixed by developments in American national security policy during the 1969-1970 period, not by United Nations attempts to settle the conflict. It was through American initiative and persuasion that the dramatic events of late July took place, including the apparent agreement by the parties to leave the issue of peace and withdrawal fluid, not in terms of ultimate principle but in terms of negotiating maneuver. And it was to the United States that the Middle East looked after the cease-fire began for further hints as to where the new opening would lead. What took place, instead of intense American diplomatic activity to move toward new phases of settlement, was the resumption of talks with Ambassador Jarring. Predictably, the forces of inertia assumed ritualized poses.

Civil War in Jordan

In the seemingly endless struggle between the Arabs and Israel, the predominant actors have usually been various national states in the Middle East. This has misled some observers into believing that if a peace settlement could be worked out between Israel and the established Arab governments, the issue of Israel's acceptance among the Arabs would be solved. This is wishful thinking. Despite spasmodic warfare that has brought death, destruction and sometimes loss of territory to the Arab states surrounding Israel (Syria, Lebanon, Jordan and Egypt), the chief victims have not been national combatants but those uprooted and made stateless by Israel's rise to nationhood. These are the Palestinian Arabs who have been forced to leave their homeland to dwell in refugee camps in surrounding Arab lands and in Gaza. Recalling Jewish experience in Europe during the 20th century and for centuries before, Israel's very existence is an assertion that there is no worse human fate than to lose one's citizenship, to become stateless. In former United States Chief Justice Warren's words, citizenship is "the right to have rights," its punitive withdrawal a "cruel and unusual punishment." [13] No greater danger exists for any peace settlement in the Middle East than the anger

---

[13] Trop v. Dulles, 356 U.S. 100-102 (1958); Perez v. Brownell, 356 U.S. 64 (1958). For a discussion of the relationships between citizenship and personal identity, see Robert J. Pranger, *The Eclipse of Citizenship* (New York: Holt, Rinehart and Winston, 1968), *passim*.

and despair of almost two million Palestinians who look forward to a return to their homeland which they now see as "occupied" by Israel. This homeland includes, in the minds of most of them, *all* of contemporary Israel and not just the Arab territories occupied in 1967. Principally a secular, socialist force, the Palestinian Resistance Movement adamantly opposes a Jewish or any other religious state in Palestine.

The Palestinian tragedy is no passing phenomenon, even for those authorities who want to deal only in government-to-government relations under the illusion that should governments settle their differences, then one can dispose of "inconvenient" problems such as the stateless Palestinians. This is an illusion because it is precisely this statelessness that makes any group of persons "inconvenient," and feeling inconvenient they think of themselves as forgotten. Those who feel forgotten have nothing to lose by desperate and violent acts. Such acts may actually call the attention of national states to the existence of Palestinians as a people rather than as an inconvenience.[14] It should also be remembered, however, that modern Israel was founded on a similar historical experience—in its case, that the Jew was inconvenient to others because of his rootlessness and thus had an obligation to himself and mankind to find roots in a national home. Against this background of intense emotional conflict between Palestinian and Israeli, which is curiously a conflict between identical principles (even extending to secularism among some of Israel's founders, though not necessarily in present state principles), emerged the civil war in Jordan during September 1970. The war was preceded by a daring and desperate act, the hijacking of four intercontinental airliners by the most leftist of the Palestinian resistance groups, the Popular Front for the Liberation of Palestine (PFLP).

A very brief account of the Palestinians, after 1948, as they developed their own national self-consciousness and "resistance movement," will provide a useful background for approaching the trouble in Jordan during September 1970. The 1947 partition of Palestine by the United Nations was opposed by Palestinian Arab paramilitary forces (paramilitary conflict between Arabs and Jews in Palestine was, by then, a way of life). However, Israel's resounding victory in 1948 left these Arabs either as "refugees" outside Israel's borders or as sullen residents within Israel, but in either case without national

---

[14] That they may have nothing to gain either is never easily appreciated by the most extreme ideologists in any movement.

citizenship.[15] The 1967 war made matters worse. Although a number of Palestinians have become citizens of other Arab states (few could be full citizens of Israel under the religious strictures at the base of Israel's law of citizenship), almost all Arabs who claimed Palestine as their past or present home identified themselves with the dream of returning to Palestine and to what they felt to be their homeland. Indeed, with the reinvigoration of the resistance movement in the 1960s, certain Palestinians returned from abroad to join the struggle under *noms de guerre*, with an emotional upsurge as profound as the Zionist *aliyah* (ascent) to Israel. After the 1948 defeat, neither refugee camps nor second-class national status in Israel nor acquired first-class citizenship in another Arab state or somewhere else could erase this Palestinian irridentism. For American policy after 1948, hated by most Palestinian leaders no matter what tack it would follow, the Palestinian question became primarily a refugee problem. Only in the last few years has this policy talked of the "legitimate aspirations" of the Palestinian "people." [16]

The Suez War of 1956 provided impetus for establishing the Palestine National Liberation Movement (*Fatah*) in 1958.[17] When the split between Egypt and Syria in 1961 ended their union as "The United Arab Republic," many Palestinians became convinced they could no longer rely on Arab national politics to bring Israel to defeat. Encouraged by the success of the Algerian revolution in 1962, they increasingly came to see themselves as a similar resistance movement. In 1964 the Arab states sponsored the Palestine Liberation Organization (PLO), a kind of central body to represent the Palestinians in their dealings with other Arab states in inter-Arab affairs, with the Palestine Liberation Army (PLA) as its military organization. By 1965 *Fatah* was beginning direct military operations against Israel, which gave this group special ascendancy in the PLO and PLA. The operations of these organizations were financed from Arab national treasuries.

Following the humiliating Arab defeat in the 1967 war, the PFLP emerged as a left-wing competitor in the movement. Despite this competition, *Fatah* worked strenuously during 1968 and 1969 to

---

[15] Having sponsored partition, the United Nations then established refugee camps under UNRWA auspices, liberally supported by the United States who was Israel's chief backer.

[16] See President Nixon's *U.S. Foreign Policy for the 1970's: A Report to the Congress* (February 25, 1971), p. 129.

[17] At the essence of "fatah" is a rich Arabic word, *fath*, which denotes capture, victory, opening of the gates of profit, inspiration, new beginnings.

capture leadership, with its chief, Yasir Arafat, becoming chairman of the PLO Executive Committee in February 1969. Under Arafat, the PLO came into closer contact with Arab governments, including those conservatively inclined, and more money was contributed to PLO operations. The PFLP held out against this united organization until February 1970, when it joined a new Unified Command with *Fatah* and eight other groups. Although a united program was agreed to by this command, and a central committee of all ten commando (*fedayeen*) organizations [18] was created in June 1970, the tensions between *Fatah* and PFLP were never really settled. This stress among the various groups constituting the Central Committee of the PLO, especially the strain between *Fatah* and PFLP, was nevertheless overshadowed by the conflict between various *fedayeen* groups and the governments of Jordan and Lebanon, over the rights of these groups under local law, culminating in the insurrection in Jordan during September. Nevertheless, the hijacking of aircraft and other similar, desperate acts were the work of PFLP. Although *Fatah* and its closest allies engaged in numerous terrorist activities against Israel, as well as paramilitary actions in Jordan and Lebanon, there was not the same ideological extremism about the activities of most of the members of the PLO that there was with the PFLP.[19] After all, if one of the points of dramatic resistance was to gain international sympathy for the Palestinians, then acts committed against innocent citizens of other nations would be detrimental to the movement's interest.

In sum, Palestinian irridentism had developed from despair in the refugee camps, to reliance on Arab governments, to a resistance movement with various shades of ideology. Although the primary target of the movement was Israel, the organization's base of operations was two-pronged, from Jordan and Lebanon, with right of transit but no residency granted (or, indeed, encouraged) by Syria. Propaganda emanated from Cairo until restrictions were imposed in 1970. Arms aid and direct military support were confined to Iraq and Syria after the August 1970 cease-fire (these two states had rejected the cease-

[18] One who sacrifices himself recklessly, especially for his country is *fidā'i*; *fidā'iya* is a spirit of self-sacrifice.

[19] This has led some, mistakenly, to refer to the more "moderate" policies of *Fatah*. True, within the movement there are differing tactical positions, but the basic, burning issue of Palestinian national consciousness remains common for *all* groups. Being a human as well as political (in the narrow sense of political maneuver) question, the demand for consciousness remains quite uncompromising, hence "radical." Still, the United States can—and should—deal with it as a matter of national policy, as the recommendations at the end of this study suggest.

fire). By far the greatest impact of the PLO was not on Israel, however, but on Jordan: constant tension and a series of armistices between King Hussein's government and the *fedayeen* culminated in airline hijackings and insurrection during September.

Turning to King Hussein's government, in the long acrimonious struggle with various *fedayeen* organizations the king maintained his power over the Hashemite Kingdom of Jordan. A soft-spoken young man by temperament, Hussein found himself embroiled in heady Arab and Jordanian politics, as well as war with Israel, for almost two decades before 1970, during which time he had learned that his country's survival as a poor state truncated in the 1967 war required firm control as well as artful maneuver. Against the uncompromising *fedayeen*, who disputed his claim that he was the sole ruler in Jordan—of both native residents and Palestinians alike—Hussein devised a policy that combined both force and art. As it turned out, he not only survived, he triumphed in his bloody encounters with the *fedayeen* in September 1970.

King Hussein was also the strongest supporter of American peace initiatives in the Middle East. Of the three Arab powers bested by Israel in 1967, Egypt and Syria deserted the United States in a cloud of angry recrimination and broken relations; Jordan did not. Perhaps because his nation suffered so much after 1967 in the waves of Israeli aerial retaliation for *fedayeen* attacks from Jordanian bases,[20] perhaps because he was a firm friend of the United States, or perhaps for a combination of these and other reasons, he agreed to the cease-fire in late July despite *fedayeen* threats that they would break his government. He also set his army to work controlling commando activity in the cease-fire's wake and even before.

As often is the case, those who protest loudest for peace are not always its most effective friends: this unassuming Arab monarch cared so much for a peace he thought would save his nation from being ground to bits between Israel and the Palestinians that he would use force to this end. But first he would have to save himself.[21] Threatened in September, initially by the *fedayeen* and then by Syrian intervention on their behalf, Hussein turned to his own resources and then to the United States for assistance. American decisions were made to answer promptly and positively his requests for moral sup-

---

[20] Without an adequate air defense and radar warning system, Jordan's villages and towns were defenseless against Israel's rapid deployment of attack aircraft.

[21] The King's own personal survival was at issue too. He could not forget his grandfather, Abdullah, the founder of modern Jordan, who died at an assassin's hands. Nor was the regicide in Iraq in 1958 forgotten.

port, arms and medicine, in the belief that if Hussein lost his throne, all chances for sustaining the cease-fire and moving beyond it would be lost. This was not a classic American intervention in the "Cold War" tradition; no one intimately involved within the United States government thought the question of halting communism was the issue. The American objective was to protect any and every government that supported a cease-fire and eventual peace. This point is worth emphasizing: United States efforts on Hussein's behalf in September 1970 represented a maneuver for the sake of protecting actual American peace initiatives already underway. This was no "war is peace" exercise. Whatever the justice of Palestinian claims, there was felt to be a higher justice in an American peace policy that would, no doubt, include the Palestinians. (The last point was not made clear because only vague sentiments existed at the time.) Furthermore, and perhaps more important, world peace may well have been at stake: Hussein's fall could have triggered a chain of explosive events leading to major warfare in the Middle East and possibly beyond.

American involvement in the civil crisis that threatened to destroy Jordan as a national state reached its apogee in September. During June, however, fighting took place between the Palestinian guerrillas and Jordanian forces, culminating in 60 foreigners being held hostage in Amman's Intercontinental Hotel, Major Robert Perry of the United States Embassy being killed in his home by *fedayeen* on June 10, and some Americans and other nationals being evacuated from Jordan in the midst of the strife. Fighting stopped when King Hussein yielded to commando demands that he dismiss two high-ranking officers accused of working with the United States against the Palestinian cause. United States intervention was confined to making arrangements for evacuation of American citizens. Although an armistice was signed on July 10 between Hussein's government and the commandos, Jordan's agreement to the American cease-fire proposal late in July brought the conflict back to the surface.

Throughout the first eight months of 1970, aircraft hijacking and bombing incidents had sporadically taken place in Europe, with serious loss of life in the crash of two airliners bombed in flight during February (one Austrian and one Swiss). All attacks had been claimed by the PFLP. But no prior action prepared the world for the desperate acts by the PFLP on September 6 when three international airliners, two American and one Swiss, were hijacked; a British aircraft was taken three days later as well. Three of the airliners were forced to land on Jordan's remote Dawson Strip, and the fourth, a Pan American Boeing 747, was blown up at Cairo airport on the day of its capture after the passengers had deplaned. Travelers on the three aircraft hijacked to Dawson Strip were held hostage against release of certain Palestinians confined in Europe and Israel for the earlier aircraft incidents. Commandos at the airfield threatened to demolish the airplanes with their passengers on board, if these demands were not met. For 20 anxious days, until the last hostages were released, the United States awaited the results of Red Cross and Red Crescent attempts to mediate the release of the passengers. These efforts were finally successful. The downed aircraft could not be reached by Jordanian troops surrounding Dawson Strip, for fear the passengers would be killed by the PFLP. Eventually, the hostages were removed by PFLP personnel from the planes and the aircraft were destroyed as a symbolic gesture. By September 29 the last of the captured passengers had been released.

The task of freeing the hostages was complicated by the armed insurrection waged by the entire PLO organization against King Hussein beginning on September 17, the day after the PLO had readmitted the PFLP to its ranks after earlier condemning its extremism. Banking on Jordanian support for a peace settlement, the United States began a series of intricate maneuvers designed to support the King while refraining from direct intervention. The moves were considered absolutely essential to protect American national interests riding on the cease-fire and possible additional steps toward peace. Hussein's role in the cease-fire was critical, Palestinian resistance adamant: under these circumstances, the United States had only one option, support of Hussein. Palestinian control of Amman would have meant that the cease-fire would collapse on the Jordanian front when Jordan disappeared as a national entity. Then Iraq (already with some 20,000 troops in Jordan) and Syria would be tempted to intervene to control the new state. Israel might find this situation—or even a less threatening Palestinian control of northern Jordan—intolerable. Hence war between Israel and the Arabs could erupt once again along the Jordan River—and perhaps all the way to Amman and Damascus, as well as into southern Lebanon where the *fedayeen* would also be active. All this would fulfill ideological prophecies, made by Palestinian leaders and other Arab extremists, that peace in the Middle East was impossible as long as Israel existed as a Jewish state. As usual, however, the ideologues were busy fulfilling their own prophecies. Egypt's reaction to this chain of events would be critical. The risks inherent for the entire Middle East in this ambiguity seemed obvious: Soviet intervention could follow on the heels of resumed hostilities between Israel and Egypt along the Suez Canal combined with Israeli strikes eastward into Jordan.[22] War between the United States and the U.S.S.R. was not inconceivable if this scenario played to its grim conclusion.

For one week from September 17 to 24, this hypothesized chain of events threatened. American support for Hussein was deemed by Washington to be absolutely essential so that peace might be served in the face of the enormous inertial force of Palestinian hatred that apparently knew no limits at this point in time. Under conditions of civil war in Jordan, this powerful force, which paradoxically worked to strengthen the status quo so that its own revolution might proceed on course, threatened to sweep the world into war. Such are the dynamics of despair when statelessness is linked to an ideology of armed revolution! The American purpose was to halt this dynamism long enough to bring stable relations to the region by means of a policy that aimed to improve government-to-government relationships first and the Palestinian lot second. That this policy was illusory, it may be argued; that it was unprincipled, never. Actually, the Palestinians have never been convinced (a) that there exists a higher justice than their legitimate national aspirations and (b) that United States policy seeks a just peace in the Middle East instead of an Israeli oppression.

As the fighting intensified, the United States government took various actions designed to strengthen King Hussein's hand in dealing first with Palestinian insurgency and then with the intervention of Syrian military units: Sixth Fleet forces were moved and augmented (closely observed by the Soviet Union's Mediterranean naval squadron); units in Europe and at Fort Bragg, N. C. were alerted; medical supplies were shipped to Jordan for treatment of casualties, in response to King Hussein's request; and Syria was publicly warned against extending its intervention in Jordan. Later in the year, King Hussein discussed new American military assistance with President Nixon during his December visit to Washington.[23]

On September 21, Hussein appealed for Big Four support. The United States hinted intervention in its show of force—but never

---

[22] Recall that Israel did confirm, on October 26, 1970, that an air battle took place between Israeli and Russian-manned Egyptian aircraft on the previous July 30, with Soviet loss of life. There was no comment from Moscow.

[23] There were also certain hints of United States intervention, one involving a White House background briefing in Chicago during the President's visit there, and carried in early editions of the *Chicago Sun-Times* of September 17. Although the newspaper withdrew this hint from its late editions, the White House remained ambiguous on possible American reactions.

directly admitted such designs, thus keeping enough ambiguity in its position to encourage flexibility on the part of the other actors; the Russians and French warned against any foreign intervention; and the British publicly expressed concern about the situation. Moscow informed both London and Washington that it had asked Syria to withdraw its invading forces from northern Jordan. Arab states other than Iraq and Syria entered the civil war as mediators, while Iraqi forces stationed in Jordan scrupulously refrained from hostile activities against Hussein. Among the Arab states, only Syria intervened, with results disastrous for itself. The PLO insurrection received full public support from the People's Republic of China.

After heavy fighting from September 23 to 25, Jordanian air and armored units chased Syrian tanks back across the frontier they had crossed on September 21. Jordanian success was insured by earlier control of the Palestinian insurrection in Amman and its environs. In every case, King Hussein's victories were his own: his armed forces showed unexpected decisiveness in their use of armor and artillery, while his tiny air force sprang to the attack against Syrian air and armored units; especially impressive was Jordan's adroit deployment of its small contingent of British-supplied Hawker Hunter attack aircraft. American posturing with various "shows of force" may have strengthened the King's hand, but the field of forces was then so fluid that it was difficult to say just what impact such gestures by the United States had on events. Reports of Israeli buildups along the Jordanian frontier were also circulated; again, the significance of such reports for Hussein's success was indeterminate. Similarly, Soviet intervention to halt Syrian incursions into Jordan may or may not have met with success.

On September 27 Hussein and Arafat signed a 14-point agreement in Cairo ending the 10-day civil war, a pact widely interpreted as a significant victory for Jordan's king. Late in 1970 fighting erupted again but, in spite of a Syrian threat to intervene, Jordan quelled the uprising. During 1971 the PLO was in a period of recuperation from its serious defeats of 1970. More important from the standpoint of American interest, the cease-fire continued between the Arabs and Israel on both the Jordan River and Suez Canal fronts, in spite of intermittent guerrilla activities against Israel and Jordan.

Looking back on American support for King Hussein, one cannot help but ponder the clash of ideals at work in that serious crisis for world order. On the one hand was the American vision of stable relations between states which would insure peace for mankind. It is silly ideology to allege, as some Arab extremists have, that American interests were simply to insure Israeli gains after the 1967 war and to shore up monarchical reaction in the Arab world. Such a view fails to give American policymakers credit for their principles as well as for their maneuvers.

On the other hand, there is the Palestinian anger and despair over statelessness, now translated into a revolutionary resistance movement armed with modern weapons and ideological doctrines. If a stable world peace is the highest of visions, so might be the belief of Palestinians that their own humanity can only be guaranteed by a national state that represents Palestinians. One principle of justice seemingly contradicts another: one side argues that only in the context of peace can the question of national justice be addressed adequately, while the other takes a position that peace is insured only when the legitimate aspirations of mankind are satisfied (recalling, among other historical documents, the Declaration of Independence). As long as these principles are thought to be mutually exclusive, all the more so because many Arabs see American peace plans as a defense of Israel's independence against Palestinian independence, then there will be war between the United States and Palestinian leadership even if thoughtful persons on all sides deplore it. It has been the policy of the United States to link these principles, but the practice of this policy has appeared to some, as in the Jordanian crisis of September, to place one or more principles above justice for the Palestinians. But are these principles of peace, territorial integrity and justice as incompatible as some might insist? The recommendations at the end of this study indicate how, without any rhetorical legerde-main, these principles can be combined in a *process toward* a final peace settlement which includes principles interacting positively with each other rather than in conflict. Such an approach is possible, how-ever, only if one perceives the field of political action as a space for reconciling mutually conflicting claims to justice without ever fixing, once and for all, a hierarchical relationship between these claims. In the ideologically charged atmosphere of the Middle East, this vision proves a difficult one indeed.[24]

---

[24] The assassination of Jordanian Premier Wasfi Tal in Cairo on November 28, 1971, may add yet a new chapter to the conflict between the Palestinian Resist-ance and King Hussein. The PFLP was quick to claim credit for the murder, promising more assassinations of Arab leaders unfriendly to the Palestinian cause.

3
SITUATION IN 1971

It is perhaps significant that the key decisions made by the United States immediately after the August cease-fire were not decisions to follow this initiative with equally momentous efforts to put inertial forces to work for peace. Rather, they were decisions to deal with imminent dangers to the cease-fire. True, these decisions stemmed from events largely beyond the control of the United States. But it is also a fact that a truce, in itself, provides no more than a breathing spell for use either to move toward peace or to prepare for new warfare. A cease-fire furnishes time for opportunity, nothing else. Because no major U.S. steps were taken to shape the aftermath of the cease-fire, and with American attention riveted on possible new causes for war, it is possible that the cease-fire has metamorphosed from a peace initiative to a truce between wars.

Someone should have filled the vacuum. Between August 1970 and December 1971, new proposals came forth from all sides, the latest having been offered by a four-nation African delegation to Jerusalem and Cairo headed by Senegal's president, Léopold Senghor. The United States was also active, especially in the fall of 1971 when Secretary Rogers proposed opening the Suez Canal as the next step toward peace.[1] In the main, however, these proposals centered not on a package settlement, but rather on an "interim settlement" consisting of some formula that would combine the opening of Suez with a limited Israeli pullback from the canal. Moreover, no central actors were visible during most of 1971. For example, the United States

---

[1] In an address before the United Nations on October 4, 1971. The address was preceded by months of private American maneuvering for an "interim settlement" that would open the Suez Canal, but there was no public statement of policy by the United States regarding Suez until late in 1971.

failed, despite a much-heralded trip to the Middle East by Secretary Rogers during May, to fix the Middle East's attention on peace as it had from late 1969 until September 1970. Hence the powerful image of the United States as peacemaker that had emerged by mid-1970 lost some of its luster.

The central problem associated with opening the Suez Canal as the step beyond the cease-fire is not the step itself but the question of where it might lead.[2] The cease-fire was exciting to the principals because it truly represented a new beginning for something as yet indistinct in overall design, but the second step cannot make such a claim. In other words, steps beyond the original one have interest for what they point toward, for what kinds of total pattern they suggest. Disembodied as an isolated action, opening Suez does not appeal to the Arabs. Furthermore, embodied in an overall settlement package with no sense of timed negotiations with the Arabs, the idea is not attractive to Israel either—who would rather, given these circumstances, accept the proposal as an isolated step. Hence an impasse has been reached on opening Suez for the same reason that the cease-fire was not immediately followed by more American initiatives for peace: apparently the United States government did not articulate a timed or phased scenario, where each step could be seen in context and where all parties would be alerted to the "rules of the game" in establishing this context; at least publicly this was not done.[3] General references to Ambassador Jarring's mission or to Security Council Resolution 242 would not suffice as substitutes.

It is hard to believe that such phased scenarios were not proposed within the United States government. Yet the public proposals—particularly Mr. Rogers' address to the United Nations on October 4, 1971—seem curiously *ad hoc* rather than carefully planned. For this reason, apparently, the usual critical audience of Arabs and Israelis quickly found flaws in the American recommendations of

---

[2] Some American and Israeli military analysts see opening of the Suez Canal as troublesome for the United States, because it would give strategic advantage to the U.S.S.R. Unfortunately for this view, the arena of political relationships is not a mechanical place with strategic stoppers for naval bathtubs; strategic advantage is gained first *within* the field of relationships (however fleeting this advantage), not in geography. The Soviet Union has geographical advantage in the Eastern Mediterranean today because of its close relations with Egypt and other Arab states, and not vice versa. This argument does not deny the legitimacy of American military concern. It only adds to this concern a reminder that the horse is already out of the barn, the door stands ajar, and closed canals are insufficient means for corralling the runaways.

[3] Obviously a public discussion of this would have to be through general references only, not in detail.

1971. Needless to say, their own peace proposals to each other (the cease-fire had at least inspired Cairo and Jerusalem to enter a war of words over such plans) were equally unacceptable. The African mission to the Middle East was active enough to secure Israel's acceptance of some of its proposals, but Arab agreement was doubtful.[4] Here again, the idea of smaller powers intervening outside the Big Four and Jarring contexts should have been addressed by the United States in August 1970 when the truce was fresh. Indeed nations east and south of Suez would be among the prime beneficiaries of a re-opened canal. Significantly, however, President Senghor saw his mission as a "last chance" for peace rather than a "new start."

Against this background, it is bootless to speak confidently of the "present situation" in late 1971 in any detail: the Middle East's kaleidoscopic energies defy definitive treatment at any time, least of all when the parties are talking of lost opportunities and last chances. The more detailed an analysis of the fleeting present, the more attention will be diverted from the all-important question of looking ahead to anticipate future events. Roughly speaking, however, the current situation looks something like the following.

On October 4, 1971, 15 months after he announced a major United States initiative to gain a cease-fire on June 25, 1970, Secretary Rogers proposed, as the step beyond the cease-fire, the opening of the Suez Canal under an interim settlement plan. Why the United States, which clearly held the diplomatic advantage in August 1970, should have waited for over one year to propose publicly a second, modest step toward peace (Mr. Rogers called it a "third step" because he considers Resolution 242 the first step) remains a mystery. There was the rumor about Dayan's position in late 1970, followed by Egypt's proposals for opening the Suez Canal in early 1971. And a burst of American private diplomatic energy apparently took place in mid-1971 dealing with the canal and an initial Israeli withdrawal.[5] If timing was a problem, virtually all major actors in the Middle East had taken a position on opening Suez long before October 1971. Perhaps the United States was distracted by the crises of late 1970 and

---

[4] Egypt succeeded in persuading African leaders to change this proposal into a United Nations resolution that called for Israel's commitment to full withdrawal from Arab territories occupied in 1967 before commencement of a new mission by Ambassador Jarring. The resolution was passed by the General Assembly on December 13, 1971, with Israel opposed and the United States in abstention.

[5] One version of the details was revealed by President Sadat in an interview in *Newsweek* (December 13, 1971), pp. 43-47. See also his interview with C. L. Sulzberger on December 10 in the *New York Times* (December 13, 1971).

the controversy with Israel over supply of additional Phantom jets in 1971. But the 1970 peace initiatives were forged in the midst of frenetic events, with escalatory warfare a daily reality, and the Phantom question provided a painful dilemma in 1970 as well as in 1971.[6] Finally, the idea that Ambassador Jarring would move into the breach right after August 8, 1970 has already been discussed, but at best this could explain only several months' delay in new initiatives. In short, the impetus toward peace seemed to wane in late 1970 and throughout 1971, despite signs of moderation in Egypt, Jordan, the Sudan and Syria.[7] Time was fast running out, as the African peace mission warned in late 1971. Hyperbole this warning may have been, but Egypt's President Sadat *had* set the end of 1971 as a deadline and reports were circulating in mid-November that the U.S.S.R. was fearful that Egypt would implicate Moscow in renewed hostilities with Israel.

While Israel's ambassador to the United States was indirectly confirming, on November 11, that his country had proposed to the United States an opening of the Suez Canal without any Israeli pull-back, President Sadat was making a major address to the newly elected People's Assembly in Cairo on the same date. Sadat affirmed that his February 4, 1971 offer to clear the Suez Canal was still open, but that the real problem was "the occupied territory and the rights of the Palestinian people," and not the canal. He called for Israel's accept-ance of Resolution 242 and promised that before 1972 he would determine a course of war against Israel if a political settlement were not achieved. Egypt could not continue, he was suggesting, in a state of no peace, no war. Such a "fate-determining decision" would be based on "the right time, the right circumstances and with the right means." [8] Absent for over one year, fate had resumed its active role in the Middle East's field of forces.

Perhaps even more discouraging for those who believed in 1970 that American Middle East policy—and, beyond that, all American foreign policy—should be motivated by independent creativity in the service of national interests was the appearance of official and unoffi-cial expressions of American concern over "the growing Soviet threat"

[6] One could argue that if the United States had immediately pressed forward after August toward opening Suez, the Phantom issue could have been settled, to Israel's satisfaction, as part of the overall phasing of the settlement process with no Arab animosity. Nevertheless, the public request on June 2, 1971 by Israel for more Phantoms seemed ill-timed in light of Mr. Rogers' peacemaking visit to Israel and Egypt less than a month earlier.

[7] Events in the Sudan verged on providing significant opportunities for strength-ening American interests there in the midst of Soviet misfortunes.

[8] *New York Times* (November 12, 1971).

in the Mediterranean and Indian Ocean. For some, the main confrontation in the wake of a smashing American diplomatic victory in 1970, which was loudly applauded throughout the world, was worse than ever (as if such success were too incredible to believe): now the chief issue would be an American struggle with the U.S.S.R. in the Middle East for the world balance, with Israel's survival at stake. How a truce, which replaces senseless warfare with fragile time for reassessment of maximal claims, could be a worse situation for American interests than what preceded that truce represents one of those mysterious closed circles in Cold War logic.

As is well known, however, the *petitio principii* in logic clouds rational assessment of any problem, just as it mindlessly sends nations to war. Soviet policy in the Middle East continues to be one of uninhibited patronage of Arab causes, as in the Treaty of Friendship with Egypt in May 1971, with the net result that in the absence of countervailing American gains among the Arabs, the Soviet threat to American interests *does* grow. But to find out how to improve one's position in the Middle East, one must cease being frantic about the Russians and address instead the problem of Arab allegiances. In other words, Cold War logic hides more than it reveals, binds American policy to outcomes rather than beginnings, and all this the U.S.S.R. gladly encourages in the condescending spirit of Pavlov for his poor dog. One cannot blame Israel for capitalizing on the Pavlovian responses at work between the United States and the U.S.S.R.: because Israel really is faced with a physical Soviet threat and it cares nothing much for Arab sympathy, it also encourages the United States to think exclusively about the U.S.S.R.

At the end of 1971, therefore, American policy toward the Middle East had developed an acute schizophrenia. To keep peace initiatives alive the United States would have to maintain an independent course in a policy field of asymmetrical relationships. At the same time, however, the Soviet Union had the option, with its peerless access to Arab capitals, of "upping the stakes" in the Arab-Israel competition, thus forcing the United States away from an independent course with credit to itself and into a dependent policy contingent on the policies and prophecies of others. (This option is always open to the Arabs and Israel also.) *In extremis* such dependence would assume the familiar terminology of the Cold War, never a good substitute for a formidable American policy based on initiatives with which *others* would have to wrestle. That the U.S.S.R. might threaten Israel's national security could not be doubted, nor could the obvious dedication of the United States to protecting Israel's integrity, but this was only one of several major problems confronting the United States in the Middle East. Another problem salient everywhere in the world, but no place more than in the Middle East, was the making of a strong, vital American foreign policy that would bring peace to the world and honor to the United States. If Israel's defense falls under the responsive (and now Cold War) category, the making of peace in the Middle East belongs under the initiatory category. These two categories are not mutually exclusive, but neither are they identical. The recommendations that follow are an attempt to work these responsive and initiatory principles together into a consistent, if not homogeneous, proposal for peace.[9]

---

[9] Other ideologies were active toward the end of 1971 also, as the assassination of Jordanian Prime Minister Tal in Cairo on November 28 indicates.

4
CONCLUSIONS AND
RECOMMENDATIONS

Early in this study it was argued that, speaking in general terms, it is useful to see foreign policy as a complicated and fluid field of reasons, decisions, policies, results and assessments. Asymmetry among policies and disjunction between events become commonplace, while traditional linear images of cause and effect, as well as stimulus and response, lose much of their relevance. In such situations it becomes rather pointless to speak about national security policy as dominating the field or keeping a status quo intact; instead, policy becomes more an exploratory enterprise, with no special powers of transcendence. Factors of judgment *within the midst* of events would become more important than factors of control over events. Here the image of a political leader as explorer rather than demigod is fitting.

Nevertheless, within this field larger states command more resources for exploring their interests than smaller states. Among these resources is the respect smaller powers demonstrate for greater powers. Superpowers with the strength of the United States and the Soviet Union occupy particularly advantageous positions within the field of international affairs, in terms of moving their policies forward to desired outcomes. These special positions seldom yield transcendental power, so that one might speak of a state "dominating" or "being in ascendancy over" the field. But, on the other hand, such positions do afford unique opportunities and special responsibilities.[1]

---

[1] While military power is not the *sine qua non* of "superpower" status, it is one of several fundamental conditions necessary for such status. Hence, those who desire that the United States exercise special responsibilities for peace as well as war in world affairs, on the basis of its superpower status, would seemingly continue to support the significant military preparedness necessary, in part, for such status.

It is out of these opportunities and responsibilities, always marginally superior but superior nevertheless to other states, that there develops world leadership in international affairs. Yet such advantages are mere potentials unless nations, such as the United States, create policies that match opportunities—that is, unless they live up to their responsibilities.

During 1969 and 1970, the Middle East provided at one and the same time a field of seemingly intractable forces locked in escalatory warfare and a field that paradoxically afforded special opportunities for the United States to expand its influence in the region. A new national administration, early identified with a balanced policy regarding the Arabs and Israel, moved from this posture to create a policy balanced in another respect—that of mixing principle, maneuver and timing in order to capitalize on unique opportunities to make a peace that would protect its interests in Israel and the Arab world. Creative policy that initiates as well as reacts, however, requires enormous effort; such effort was expended within the United States government during the first nine months of 1970 as the entire National Security Council system (comprising State, Defense, CIA and the NSC staff) worked to forge a political and military policy that achieved significant results for peace by August 1970. Unfortunately, for many tangled reasons, lassitude has subsequently crept back to prominence in the policy field, so that the cease-fire may drift toward war unless new initiatives are undertaken.

Aside from the lessons for national security policy in general, lessons remaining to be explored in greater depth, the American decisions regarding the Middle East in 1969 and 1970 also prove instructive for peacemaking in a more philosophic sense. No nation has the power to "make peace" by unilateral fiat. To accomplish such a feat, where one nation becomes lawgiver and arbiter of the destiny of all others, would require an imperial system constructed along the lines of ancient Rome. *Pax Augustus* was possible because the scope of international relations was, to a considerable extent, domesticated as the internal jurisdiction of a single power under an "empire." Travelers in the first century A.D. could use Roman roads from Spain to Egypt, in the process enjoying a single coinage and language plus the comfort of armed protectors under a unified command. But the powers of such universal law no longer belong to any single people, nor do the unilateral capabilities to keep universal peace.

War is much easier to make by unilateral action than peace. War constitutes a tangible gesture wherein one state visibly attacks another, thus making that state an "enemy." Peace, on the other hand, is largely a persuasive exercise with few tangible points of leverage, unless one means by peace a dictated settlement following war. No armies, except peacekeeping forces, are at its disposal; vast budgets are not required to move its interests; and only the most militant pacifist would talk of a "peace attack" on other powers (unilateral disarmament may be a more common variant of this). What is required for peace, however, is plenty of human ingenuity.

Obviously, when nations perceive their interests to lie in the direction of peace, as the United States does in the Middle East, then the total resources of the state, including military force, may become devoted to preventing war. For such a perception to develop, a special fascination with persuasion rather than force must be present. Some have suggested, at times vehemently, that if an entire social and government system of a nation, such as the United States, could be reformed so that it would be peaceably inclined, then it would, by its new internal dynamics, bring its entire energy to bear for this end in the field of international affairs. Many panaceas have been proposed, ranging from abolition of governmental secrecy to wholesale revolution. All such nostrums belong to the realm of those who believe, for various reasons, that the United States can domesticate the international sphere to such an extent that its law will become universal. Perhaps this stems from a widely prevalent view that the United States is "imperialistic" and thus rules an "empire" in the Roman tradition. If so, yet another *petitio principii* is at work, simply the reverse side of the same coin on which is imprinted the image of Cold War logic—and indeed fashioned in reaction to the latter image. In its entirety, however, the coin represents a vision of American dominance in the field of international policy, the ideal of a predestined national transcendence over events which cannot exist. Out of the masterful images of American foreign policy since 1945 have developed not only Cold War demonology but Anti-War eschatology, in both cases based on the same illusory *Pax Americana*.

The answer to the question, "How does a perception that peace is in the American national interest develop?" is found only in the field of policy. Such a perception cannot be legislated; it cannot be dictated. It must be *discovered in the process of persuasion itself*. And in such discovery, especially when maps and instruments are still crude, lies danger of responsibility and risk. Those involved in the search for national interest, a search conducted *within* the tangled policy field and not in sanitized compartments of analysis, may find war as well as peace. No absolutes exist here, only shifting relationships among policies and interests giving some nations *greater* opportunities and responsibilities, in certain historical periods, than other nations. If peace is finally discovered in the Middle East, it will be the result of states acting in concert with each other for often contradictory reasons, even though the balance could just as easily have tipped to local and even world war. In this tentative search, limits to action are always present but always imprecise; if the discovery of peace is not accidental, it is not entirely a matter of fixed purpose either. In the end, principled men and women make both war and peace, not merely because of their principles but also because of how they move their purposes within the contingent field of international relations. Explorer and artist merge perspectives here: purpose encounters paradox, initiative meets reflection, consistency finds contradiction, realism follows image, and triumph flirts with tragedy.

Recommendations

Renewed fighting between the Arab states and Israel could only work adversely on American interests in the Middle East, especially if the United States were drawn into the conflict directly on Israel's behalf so that American forces engaged Arab and Soviet forces. One can only imagine the impact of such intervention on American fortunes in the Arab world for the next decades, to say nothing of the combined effect that U.S.-U.S.S.R. hostilities would have on world peace. For this reason, the United States has only one policy option open that is not totally irresponsible—to continue its peace initiatives in a policy of balanced principle and maneuver, despite increasingly pessimistic views from other actors that a new period of warfare is on the horizon.

With this in mind, Secretary Rogers proposed opening the Suez Canal, as part of an interim settlement plan, to the United Nations on October 4, 1971. A fair approach, he argued, would contain two basic principles: (1) that an interim settlement is "merely a step toward complete and full implementation of Resolution 242 within a reasonable period of time and not an end in itself," and (2) that neither side can expect to achieve "as part of an interim agreement, complete agreement on the terms and conditions of an over-all settlement."

In the remainder of his proposal, although he addressed other issues (cease-fire continuation, withdrawal zone, supervisory arrangements, an Egyptian presence east of the canal, and use of the waterway), the secretary did not clarify his two basic principles sufficiently to allay the fears of the other actors as to how their national security interests would be affected in the interim settlement. This was especially true for Israel who was also locked in a controversy with the United States over more Phantom jets. Whatever may have been communicated to Israel and Egypt privately in explication of the secretary's U.N. address (private consultations were underway), it appears from what was publicized that the latest American plan has left the issue of how Suez fits into a wider peace settlement unnecessarily ambiguous. Indeed, it seems obvious that the two basic principles were designed to apply "even-handed" tactics to Egyptian and Israeli fears: one points toward Resolution 242, for Egypt's benefit, and the other says an interim settlement would not contain a complete agreement, for Israel's satisfaction.[2]

Two days later, Egyptian Foreign Minister Riad, insisting before the same U.N. forum that any Suez pact must contain an Israeli pledge to pull out of occupied territories, made no reference to Mr. Rogers' October 4 address.[3] Some reports then circulated that Riad's oversight was due to extremely delicate negotiations between Egypt and the United States. But it could just as easily have been the result of Egypt's reading the speech and finding nothing new in the "basic principle" provided for its consumption. In fact, Riad's statement that Israel must give a withdrawal pledge *within* the interim settlement agreement could have been designed to telescope interim and final settlement in a way that Mr. Rogers had, in fact, ruled out as unrealistic.[4]

While Foreign Minister Riad ignored Mr. Rogers' October 4 address, Israel's prime minister deplored it for having allegedly shifted the U.S. position to the point where the United States now was backing Egypt on the issue of opening the canal (to wit: duration of cease-fire fixed, Egyptian troops permitted across the canal, and interim settlement integrated into overall plan). She insisted that the new plan was contrary to assurances given her earlier by Secretary Rogers and by Assistant Secretary of State Sisco.[5]

There is another possibility, however. It may be that Riad ignored the American proposal and Mrs. Meir opposed it because they were not very clear just where the United States intended to go in terms of carefully planned and phased initiatives that would capitalize on the

---

[2] Text in *New York Times* (October 5, 1971).

[3] *New York Times* (October 7, 1971).

[4] A point reiterated by President Sadat on November 11, *New York Times* (November 12, 1971).

[5] Statement by Prime Minister Golda Meir on October 26, *New York Times* (October 27, 1971).

cease-fire.[6] In the hope that at least the United States has some sense of direction, even if it cannot communicate this to the other actors in the Middle East policy field, the following recommendations are made. Indeed, the other actors may be confused in part because the United States did not forcefully seize the diplomatic initiative it held in August 1970 in an attempt to give a better picture, during the months immediately following, of where and how it thought the region might search for further initiatives.

To begin with, it is important to review briefly two fundamental issues constantly raised by Israel and Egypt (who will be treated here as "proxy" for the other Arab states) regarding peace settlement plans. The Israelis have insistently argued that the most tangible step toward peace they could identify would be direct negotiations with the Arabs. Here is the *sine qua non*, the crucial symbol of Arab good faith, the ultimate guarantee that Israel could hope to live at peace with its neighbors. As late as September 30, 1971, in addressing the United Nations, Israel's foreign minister proposed that he and the Egyptian foreign minister meet in New York City to discuss opening the Suez Canal, a suggestion that met, predictably, with Arab derision.[7] That it has not encouraged the Arabs through deeds as well as words, and that "deeds" would involve more flexibility on Israel's part, has been a serious flaw in Israel's foreign policy (for example, on issues involving Jerusalem). Nevertheless, a central preoccupation for Israel during all peace settlement plans since 1948 has been the issue of what evidence can exist to indicate the Arabs really want peace— in any sense of recognizing Israel's territorial integrity—when they refuse to negotiate directly with Israel. This issue of Arab intentions is quite different from a truce observance where fighting temporarily stops for reasons of convenience, or from general assurances by Arab leaders that peace with Israel is desirable.

On the other hand, the Egyptians have argued that peace plans should be well-integrated, pointing beyond the cease-fire and the opening of the Suez Canal toward a complete settlement involving Israel's withdrawal from all the occupied territories. As President Sadat puts it, "The problem is the occupied territory and the rights

---

[6] That Mrs. Meir stays very close to the public address by Secretary Rogers in her critique may indicate that nothing further, in the way of clarification, was communicated to her. Hence, the secretary's speech to the United Nations may offer a good indication of where American thinking stood in mid-November 1971.

[7] *New York Times* (October 1, 1971). Derision, because of Arab insistence that Israel first commit itself to withdrawal.

of the Palestinian people."[8] In addition, the phases of this settlement should be accompanied by an actual Israeli withdrawal in stages. This remains a very critical issue for Egypt, because just as Israel wants direct negotiations with the Arabs as earnest for its security, so the Arabs adamantly demand to know, and then see proof of, Israel's plans for withdrawal.

The present United States plan unnecessarily skirts these two critical issues, at least in public. By avoiding them, the plan cannot capitalize on their potential for peace, and indeed, may have laid bare their potential for war. Thus, it seems an ill-conceived decision has been made: being explosive subjects likely to churn the waters, these issues are to be either postponed or ignored entirely through ambiguous terminology and indirect mediation. Then the forces of inertia never will have to face the full implications of their own inertia or can confront such hard realities late in the negotiations. Unfortunately, both sides may recognize this postponement and play the charade until their interests dictate that they break the cease-fire and return to war. If neither side has to provide an earnest of its peaceful intentions, then there is no real guarantee for peace at all.[9] Under these circumstances, the cease-fire, for all its rhetoric about peace, may even at this point in time be an interlude heralding a much more dangerous war than the one that preceded it.[10]

A peace proposal that will include both direct Arab negotiations with Israel and phased Israeli withdrawal will be considered here. At least by dealing with these emotion-packed issues once and for all, one can ascertain just how serious the Arabs and Israel are about a peace settlement. The following proposals will operate on the assumption that American peace initiatives in the Middle East have worked best when they have used inertial forces to speed rather than retard settlement. But the employment of such forces is critical. At the same time, however, compromise will not be demanded of fundamental principles: what will have to be adjusted is Israel's opposition to a settlement plan that looks ahead to the specifics of its withdrawal and Egypt's determination not to enter direct talks with Israel at an early stage in negotiations. Both sides gain from the other's concession, but nothing basic is sacrificed.

---

8 *New York Times* (November 12, 1971).

9 Without these indications, the idea that any other powers can "guarantee" a settlement seems illusory.

10 This is not to be critical of the cease-fire per se, but only to raise the matter of how time was used during the truce.

The proposed plan would start with the interim opening of the Suez Canal and an Israeli announcement that a thin-out of its forces on the canal's east bank is planned. But these initial steps would be placed within the context of an overall *timed* plan, which is not the case at present. The timing would be as follows.

Before any negotiations start, the cease-fire would be renewed for one year, with automatic renewal for another year if conditions cited below materialize. This first year would be seen as comprising four quarters, each constituting a phase in a process toward a draft peace treaty between the Arabs and Israel that would be completed or well underway at the end of the year. Only if the draft treaty were moving forward at an acceptable pace would the cease-fire be renewed again. In a protocol, signed by all major actors in the Middle East policy field, the following specifics of the plan would be accepted as constituting the "rules of the game" by which negotiations on details would progress within the one- or two-year time period.[11] An outline of the protocol appears in the Appendix.

At the start of *Phase 1* (the first three months of the plan), the Suez Canal clearing operation would commence. In addition, Israel would announce its contemplated withdrawal from the canal's east bank. Such a withdrawal would take the form of thinning out its forces within a 40-kilometer strip along the canal and would actually commence during Phase 1, contingent upon Arab agreement in advance to start negotiations in Phase 2 with the aim of proceeding from indirect to direct talks during the second three months.[12] The Egyptians would, in turn, not only announce that the clearing operation was underway, but would also state that Israel would have the right of free passage when the canal was opened (approximately six months from the beginning of the new cease-fire).

---

[11] Soviet cooperation in this plan is desirable, though not essential. With its growing power in the Arab world, however, the Soviet Union could thwart any negotiated settlement sponsored by the United States. It will be assumed here, without arguing over how "realistic" this assumption is, that Soviet support should be encouraged: in the other numerous areas of negotiation between the United States and the U.S.S.R., there should be room for enough American concessions on issues not vital to national interests to ensure the success of new American efforts for peace in the Middle East. At various points in the plan, where Soviet cooperation would be necessary but not forthcoming, footnotes will indicate possible alternatives.

[12] It should be noted that such withdrawal would begin only in the context of a protocol in which the Arabs would guarantee, in advance, negotiations commencing in Phase 2. Withdrawal in Phase 1, therefore, would be the first stage of withdrawals to be repeated in subsequent phases, the latter stages contingent on actual materialization of negotiations. Hence, the first withdrawals could be a symbolic "thinning out" of Israeli forces.

At the start of *Phase 2* (the second three months of the plan), the Arabs would inform Israel privately of their intention to send negotiators to secret meetings in a neutral place, starting as either indirect or direct talks but proceeding to direct negotiations during Phase 2.[13] These talks would be held under the combined auspices of the United States, the U.N. and the Big Four. In turn, during this phase, Israel would complete its withdrawal to the 40-kilometer line, save for a limited number of combat personnel along the canal. No Egyptian personnel would cross the canal during this phase, but would wait until the opening of the canal during Phase 3 (at the end of six months or shortly thereafter). Finally, an international commission of religious and urban affairs experts would be formed in this second phase to study the Jerusalem issue for no more than six months, looking forward to combining in some way Israeli civil jurisdiction over Jerusalem with an international, religious jurisdiction over its Holy Places.

At the beginning of *Phase 3* (the third quarter of the cease-fire's first year), Egyptian civil militia (gendarmerie) would cross the Suez Canal right after it was opened to administer affairs on the east bank. However, no regular Egyptian *military* units would cross the canal until a peace treaty was formally signed and ratified (which may not occur until well into the second year of the cease-fire). Israel's remaining forces would prepare for withdrawal should a draft treaty be ready at the end of one year and, in any event, during the cease-fire's second year. Also during the early days of Phase 3, Israel would give permission for a United Nations team to visit Jerusalem pursuant to Security Council resolutions on this subject—thus accepting, in principle, U.N. interests in the civil, as well as religious, administration of the city. Palestinian representatives would be admitted to the secret negotiations now taking place directly between the Arab states and Israel. The United States and the U.S.S.R. would grant their clients all outstanding military requests; in the case of the United States this would include Israel's long lead-time procurement of additional F-4s, with the understanding that first deliveries would not commence until the draft peace treaty was ready (the U.S.S.R. would so inform its clients also, for all aircraft deliveries). If negotiations were to break

---

[13] Secrecy is preferred but probably not essential. It will be assumed that no government would enter such negotiations if it feared being embarrassed by disclosure. On the other hand, disclosure at the right time late in the negotiations would be quite useful in preparing the various nations and the Palestinians for the ratification process in the second year of the plan.

down, the U.S. and U.S.S.R. would have to reassess their decisions on military assistance during this phase.[14]

At the start of *Phase 4* (the last quarter of the new cease-fire), there would be a public announcement that *direct* negotiations were underway. This announcement could be postponed or accelerated into an earlier phase; timing would be determined for maximum impact on the policy field but, in any case, consensus among the actors would be necessary prior to any public release. During Phase 4, the terms of the final settlement would be presented in secret negotiations. Roughly speaking, they would include: (a) in the Sinai, Israel would withdraw all its forces after ratification of the peace treaty, save civil police on the road from Elath to Sharm al-Shaykh and a small military garrison at Sharm al-Shaykh; and Egypt would be allowed to bring in gendarmerie and noncombat (support) military personnel (this arrangement could have a time limit, after which Israel would relinquish Sharm al-Shaykh, and Egypt would be allowed regular military personnel in the Sinai); (b) in the east, Israel would withdraw from the Golan Heights, but the district would be demilitarized under Syrian civil authorities with United Nations supervision; and (c) along the Jordan River's west bank, Israel would withdraw to the Hebron-Bethlehem-Jerusalem road, with the line north of Jerusalem determined after a Palestinian state is established on the West Bank (see below). At this point, recommendations from the international committee of experts on Jerusalem would be considered by the negotiators. Now arrangements would also be initiated for the assumption, by United Nations administration, of trusteeship of the West Bank of the Jordan River as the first step toward a Palestinian state. Later, the Palestinian leadership would agree directly with Israel on guarantees for Israel's and the new state's mutual frontiers.

At the close of the 12-month period, a treaty of peace would have been drafted (or be near completion) between the Arabs and Israel, in which the latter's right to exist (territorial integrity) would be explicitly and formally recognized. Signature and ratification would then take place within one year of this date. Thus, if the draft treaty were ready or near completion at the end of a year's time, then an automatic renewal of the cease-fire for another year would commence. Also, the United States and the U.S.S.R. would now agree to limit their military assistance programs in the Middle East to fixed annual levels.

---

[14] If the Soviet Union does not cooperate, the United States might arrange, in conjunction with Israel, to limit American shipment of arms to Israel in exchange for an Egyptian agreement to restrain its purchases of major military items.

Finally, during the cease-fire's second year, the Soviet Union would start to withdraw its military personnel from Egypt as the Israelis withdraw theirs from the Sinai.[15] Israel would agree to commence its total withdrawal from the Sinai (except Sharm al-Shaykh), the West Bank (to the line described earlier) and Golan Heights immediately upon the ratification of the treaty by all parties.

From the beginning of this plan, all the parties to the plan, including the United States and U.S.S.R., would be aware of the plan's details. The phases would constitute "rules of the game" in the form of a protocol agreed to among the parties. Both great powers would promise to devise contingency plans in case violations of the protocol should occur and to consult with each other before taking remedial action. In other words, the United States and U.S.S.R. would guarantee the viability of the negotiations but *not* the territorial viability of Israel and the Arab states (which would be accomplished, of course, in the treaty).[16] The process of negotiations itself would be essential for three reasons: (a) to insure that all details are secured; (b) to see that all parties are heard; and (c) to make sure that direct communications between the Arabs and Israel are established (which may, however, fall short of full diplomatic relations for some time). The prior agreement to this plan does not obligate any party to continuing with it when overriding national interests otherwise dictate.

---

15 This assumes Soviet support of the negotiations. Such support might be worked out between the United States and Egypt.

16 This assumes Soviet agreement. Especially for guaranteeing the success of the negotiations, it is quite obvious that such agreement is the preferred course for American policy. The question of *quid pro quo* has been addressed above.

APPENDIX

Protocol for One Year's Negotiations Between the Arab States and Israel Toward a Peace Treaty

Phase 1. Three Months (months 1-3)

A. At Start of Phase 1:

1. Renewal of cease-fire for one year, with automatic renewal for another year under certain conditions
   a. Algeria, Iraq, Sudan and Syria, as well as present parties to cease-fire
   b. Palestinians
   c. If above acquiescence impossible, then present parties to cease-fire, plus as many others as possible (alternative in text)
2. U.S.-U.S.S.R. general sponsorship of negotiations
3. Signature of protocol by all parties to cease-fire for one year's negotiations
4. Protocol constitutes rules of the game for negotiations to follow, as well as basis for draft treaty
   a. Pull-out permissible for national interest reasons
   b. U.S.-U.S.S.R. contingency plans for breakdown, with mutual consultation

B. During Phase 1:

1. Start of Suez Canal clearing by Egypt
   a. Public announcement by Egypt
   b. Announcement by Egypt of Israel's right of free passage
2. Announcement by Israel of contemplated withdrawal of forces from east bank of Suez Canal to line 40 kilometers eastward with withdrawal beginning in Phase 1.

67

Phase 2. Three Months (months 4-6)

A. At Start of Phase 2:
1. Negotiations between Arabs and Israel
   a. At first direct or indirect negotiations, but direct at some point during Phase 2
   b. At neutral place under combined United States, U.N. and Big Four auspices
2. Finish of Israeli withdrawal from Suez to 40-kilometer line with limited number of personnel still along canal

B. During Phase 2:
1. No Egyptian personnel across canal during this phase
2. International commission of religious and urban affairs experts on Jerusalem meets for no more than six months to find some combination of Israeli civil administration and international religious administration of Holy Places

Phase 3. Three Months (months 7-9)

A. At Start of Phase 3:
1. Egyptian civil (gendarmerie) forces across canal
2. Israeli permission for United Nations commission to visit Jerusalem

B. During Phase 3:
1. Palestinian representatives invited to secret negotiations with representatives of Israel and Arab states
2. American and Soviet agreement to outstanding military assistance requests from clients (including F-4s for Israel), but deliveries contingent on readiness of draft peace treaty at year's end (alternative in text)

Phase 4. Three Months (months 10-12)

A. At Start of Phase 4: public announcement that direct negotiations underway (timing flexible, earlier or later for maximum impact)

B. During Phase 4:
1. Terms of final settlement ready, roughly as follows:
   a. Israel withdrawal from Sinai, except for Sharm al-Shaykh and coastal road from Elath to Sharm al-Shaykh
      (1) Egyptian gendarmerie and military support elements in Sinai

(2) Timed arrangement with change in future
  b. Israel withdrawal from Golan Heights with demilitarized district under Syrian civil authorities and U.N. supervision
  c. Israel withdrawal from West Bank of Jordan River to line of Hebron-Bethlehem-Jerusalem (line north of Jerusalem to wait on establishment of Palestinian state)
2. Report of international commission of Jerusalem to negotiators
3. U.N. trusteeship for West Bank toward eventual establishment of Palestinian state

Second Year

A. Automatic renewal, given completion or near-completion of previous phases

B. Draft treaty guaranteeing Israel's territorial integrity and sovereignty

C. U.S.-U.S.S.R. agreement to limit annual levels of military assistance in Middle East

D. Mutual withdrawal of all Soviet and Israeli forces from Arab territory upon treaty's ratification
  1. U.S.S.R. from Egypt
  2. Israel's remaining contingents from all occupied territories save Sharm al-Shaykh and access road to Elath as well as certain areas to the east of Israel's pre-1967 boundaries

Cover and book design: Pat Taylor